The Discovery of a Missing King's Tomb
—Selections of Chinese Relics and Archaeology

Translated by
Zuo Boyang

Foreign Languages Press   Beijing

First Edition 1995

ISBN 7-119-01540-0

© Foreign Languages Press, Beijing, 1995

Published by Foreign Languages Press
24 Baiwanzhuang Road, Beijing 100037, China

Printed by Beijing Foreign Languages Printing House
19 Chegongzhuang Xilu, Beijing 100044, China

Distributed by China International Book Trading Corporation
35 Chegongzhuang Xilu, Beijing 100044, China
P.O.Box 399, Beijing, China

Printed in the People's Republic of China

Contents

The Excavation of Fossil Remains of Ape-men at Jinniushan

Han Yuqi

(1) The Folklore of Jinniushan

The fossil remains of an ape-man skull and limb fragments around the age of the Peking Man were unearthed on October 2, 1984, at Jinniushan (the Golden Cattle Mound), Yingkou County, Liaoning Province; the event aroused world attention. But how were they discovered and excavated? We are going to explain in the following:

Jinniushan is a small hillock with a circumference of only 1,240 metres, 69.3 metres above sea level, eight kilometres to the southwest of Yingkou County. To the east of it is a beautiful village, Xitiantun. Folklore has been passed since ancient times among the villagers that long, long ago there was a southern Taoist who came to the north seeking for treasure. On a May day he came to Jinniushan and determined that there was treasure in the mound. But where was the key to open the mound? In the village there lived an old woman who was growing two gourds, a big one and a small one. The Taoist offered her five taels of silver for the big gourd, which he was to fetch on the 15th of the eighth

1

moon, and she was charged with watching it well for him. The old lady became very tired watching the gourd, so on the thirteenth, she cut it down and hid it in a wardrobe. At dusk on the 15th the Taoist came and paid the cost, regretting his bargain. He opened the gourd and found a golden key. With it, the stone gate was opened, and a golden calf was found milling golden beans. However, the key was a little too weak to sustain the weight of the stone gate. In an instant, the golden key broke while the Taoist and the golden calf rushed out, and the gate closed again. The County Annals of Yingkou even noted this story.

In order to make a general survey in April 1973, the Cultural Relics Department of Liaoning Province assembled a training class at Fushun, and invited Li Chuankui of the Institute of Vertebrate Palacontology and Palaeoanthropology of the Chinese Academy of Sciences to make a report. He said that there were a lot of fossil points in the province—fossil remains had been found in Fuxin, Dashiqiao, Benxi.... Cui Dewen, a young man of 37, from Yingkou Museum, kept that in mind and questioned Li for more detailed information.

In May 1974, Cui Dewen, Zhang Senshui, et al., discovered four fossil points at Jinniushan. After 49 days of excavation, they found a lot of remnants of the Stone Age, and fossil remains of ancient mammals and other animals.

(2) A Connoisseur Sees the "Golden Cattle"

In the central part of Jinniushan there is a main

fault inclining 53° towards the northeast to form a series of sub-one grade faults, a broken belt measuring from 20 to 50 metres in width. Groundwater moving along the break, through long-time erosion, has formed a lot of caves and crevices. Among these four fossil points during the excavation of Jinniushan, Point A has been dug into six layers, to a depth of 11 metres. In the first layer are broken stones; the second layer contains broken stones and dark brown subclay; the third layer is yellow-brown subclay, in which a prehistoric rat and a small quantity of other mammals have been found; the fourth layer is light orange yellow subclay, two metres deep and abundant with the fossils of small animals; the fifth layer contains brown subclay and broken stones, in which have been discovered a large amount of fossil remains of mammals as well as a piece of possibly man-made slab and traces of the employment of fire; the sixth layer is reddish-brown breccia in which were unearthed at a depth of 4.5 metres the fossils of a variety of wolf and a large quantity of other mammals.

Through three excavations in 1975, 1976 and 1978, were discovered 30 more stone artifacts and 76 kinds of thick-jawed deer, sabre-toothed tiger, wolf varieties and other mammals. These, added to the 11 kinds of reptiles and birds found, total up to a thousand pieces of 87 varieties. Burned bones and ashes also had been found there. The report of the four excavations before 1978 has been published. In the meantime, associate professor Lü Zun'e of Beijing University, who had been teaching for 30 years and wanted a suitable site to bring postgraduates, came to Jinniushan between July and August 1980.

He looked over the mound, then went to the eastern foot to observe the sections of Point A. After the four previous excavations, the southern wall of caves had begun to appear; two sections of the northwest were still retained; part of the soil was heaped in the southeast; the western section was as deep as 11 metres, strata were distinct.... Upon watching, Lü Zun'e could not help crying out, "Isn't this a small fossil mound!" He looked round his company and said with delight, "This spot of heaps is quite typical and full of fossils, an ideal spot for students' practice."

By September of 1985, six students and county cadres guided by Lü and another teacher, Huang Yunping, started the excavation work. Point A sphere was divided into four squares, with one student and two labourers responsible for each square. Another student undertook Point C.

(3) The Fossil Remains of Ape-men Are Discovered

On the afternoon of September 27, Lü was a little late visiting the site. At the halfway point, a student hurried toward him on a bicycle. The student carefully produced a fragment of bone from a cotton ball, saying, "Teacher Lü, what bone is this?" It was a human kneecap. "When was it dug out?" "Just a little while ago." Lü marked the time—2:40 p.m. "Hurry up, screen the soil three times!" and they ran to Point A. In an instant, a human right heel, upper-tarsals, toes, wrist-bones, etc., were found.

The information caused an uproar in the village.

The next morning the news was sent to Beijing.

On the morning of the National Holiday (October 1), the Practice Team of Beijing University went to the working site as usual. For the sake of security, Professor Lü ordered withdrawal of the labourers and concentrated the team's full force on the First Square. He exhorted the students to be particularly careful in performing the excavation work. If any piece of bones couldn't be extracted, they weren't to hesitate to ask for his advice. He also arranged for a night-shift to watch the working site.

The next morning, a responsible postgraduate in the First Square, Xia Jingfeng, picked out a piece of bone as big as a walnut with fissures on it. He stood up at once and ran to Professor Lü. In the meantime, Lü Zun'e was putting specimens in order with Huang Yunping in a room on the hillside. As incredible as it may seem, he felt uneasy, as if something unusual had happened and he had to return to the site at once. Just as he stepped out of the doorway, he saw Xia rushing to him. "What is the difference between man and animal skull fissures?" Xia asked. Lü hastened to the spot, lay prone on the ground, and saw the fissure of a human skull. Lü further ordered, "If the fragments are turned upside down, reset them to the original position."

When told, Huang disbelieved her own hearing ability. "Is that true?" She threw down the specimens in her hands and ran up to the mound.

The whole village was in a turmoil. "A human skull has been discovered!" people told each other. Nearby brickfield workers, old men, and children, as well as young mothers carrying their babies, all ran up to the hill.

(4) Straining Work in Picking up the Skull

In spite of the joy, everyone knew the difficulty in splitting the ape-man's skull from rocks; they were stuck in the stone like concrete. Lü asked Yuan Jia-rong, head of another Square, to work together with Little Xia to pick up the skull. With a small chisel and hammer, they cautiously cleared the remains for two days. The superciliary ridge, eye socket, facial bone, upper jaw and teeth all had been taken out; only the base of the skull was still stuck to the rock by calcium carbonate.

In the course of time, a complete spine, ulna, ribs, metacarpi and restorable hipbones were also found in the vicinity. At the doorway of the eastern wall cave of the Third Square, horns of thick-jawed deer and piles of animal bones were also unearthed. In the Second Square there were burned ashes, burned soil and burned bones—indicating the employment of fire—as well as a large amount of human-cracked animal-bone fragments.

On the 4th, Guo Dashun of the Provincial Culture Department, Sun Shoudao of the Museum of Liaoning Province and Wang Xu of the History Institute of the Chinese Academy of Social Sciences came to Jinniushan. Lü was very delighted because Wang Xu is an expert in restoring archaeological objects. They considered five methods of picking up the skull but adopted the third. The chosen method was to reinforce the surface first by pasting paper and smearing plaster, then to moisten the calcium carbonate under the skull with alcohol and pick it up with care.

By 3:00 p.m. of the 5th, Wang led the operation, assisted by his student, Li Hongwei. The lower part of the skull was first encircled with hemp strips; then seven or eight layers of glued-paper strips of 1x3 inches were interwoven and placed on the skull one after another; and finally the whole lot was plastered over. By the time everything was ready, it was half past six in the evening, and quite dark.

At ten o'clock the next morning, team members, holding their breath, surrounded the operators Wang and Li while Lü ordered, "Start to lift it!" The fossil skull, which had lain there for half a million years, was taken from its old site. Flash cameras marked the scene at 11:01.

The discovery created a great sensation among the Yingkou people. Lü explained to them that thick-jawed deer had become extinct some two hundred thousand years before; in the fourth layer of Jinniushan, fossil remains of sabre-toothed tiger, a species of animal even older than the deer, had been found; judging from which, the present skull was at least two hundred thousand years old—as old as the Peking Man of Zhoukoudian, Beijing.

By eight o'clock in the evening of October 11th, the county chief of Yingkou, carrying the skull case in his own hands, escorted the Practice Team to the railway station.

(5) The Pleasing News is Brought to Beijing

The third day after his return to Beijing, Lü went to see Jia Lanpo and Su Bingqi with the photos. Jia, who had quit using tobacco, turned to his old comrade and said, "Mr. Lü has brought back a Golden Baby from Jinniushan. I'm breaking my fast; let me have a cigarette." Su, celebrating his 75 brithday, told Lü, "This news is the best present I could receive. You have done your work with the greatest care. This is a breakthrough in field excavation work of the Old Stone Age."

On the evening of the 16th, Lü and Huang, bringing with them a part of the limb bones, visited Wu Rukang for the authorities' appraisal. Wu said: "There's no doubt that these are human bones." Lü told him that in the same layer of soil there were thick-jawed deer fossils and that the soil accumulation was much like that of Zhoukoudian (the Peking Man site). Wu was going to be on a trip in a day or two, so the skull was taken to him the next afternoon. Wu commented, "The completeness of the discovery is as never before; it's much more complete than the Peking Man. The skull has so many teeth; so many limb bones help in the study of the ape-man's erect stance and pacing gestures. This sort of find has never been made before, in all the world!"

On August 9, 1985, the committee of specialists, Wu Rukang, Jia Lanpo, Su Bingqi, An Zhimin, Guo Dashun and Su Bai, released the following conclusions: Jinniushan Man is more progressive than Peking Man, more akin to the early intellectual man of Dali, Shaanxi. He lived around a hundred-odd to two hundred thousand years ago. The unearthed position of the soil layer has been uranium-dated to 310,000 years ago, although a totally accurate date has yet to be proved. The greatest significance of the discovery is how the completeness of the skull and the abundance of limb bones fill the blanks in this field of study, both at home and abroad. The find provides reference materials for the further study of the development from the upright-standing to the intellectual ape-men.

A Brief Comment on the Hongshan Culture

Li Jinyun

The Hongshan Culture is a Neolithic culture based in the northern and southern regions of the Yanshan Mountains. It was first discovered in 1935 at Hongshan (the Red Hills), Chifeng, Liaoning Province, hence the name. In recent years, remnants and remains sites have been found in west Liaoning and southeast Inner Mongolia, particularly the remain sites at Xishuiquan, Chifeng; the building cluster at Dongshanzui, Kezuo, Liaoning; the jadeware tomb at Hutougou, Fuxin; and the jade dragon, etc., at Sanxingtala, Wongniute Banner, Inner Mongolia. All of these have enlarged our understanding of the Hongshan Culture.

1. Dongshanzui Remain Site is situated on a tableland in the centre of a mountain ridge at the west bank of the Daling River, 50 metres above the riverbed. Excavation revealed a cluster of building sites: a 10-metre square stone-built foundation; a round-shaped base with a diameter of 2.5 metres, circled with stones; a poly-rounded stone base made up of 3 circles with diameters from 2.9 to 4 metres each.

In the square-shaped stone base there are three piles of unearthed rocks. Under the stone base there were unearthed a jade semiannular pendant, stone bullets, bone materials and pottery fragments. In the inner side of the south wall, a greenish jade "*huang*" was found. It is about 4 centimetres in length, with dragon heads at both ends. The heads have long lips and rhomboid eyes, and the dragon has a hole bored through the middle. Outside the east wall was unearthed an owl-shaped malachite tablet. The owl is taking wing; the feathers of its wings and tail are meticulously carved and lined. Like the dragon, the owl also has a hole bored through its middle. They were probably made as pendants.

Around the stone base many pottery figurines were found. Most were the fragments of limbs and trunks, but the heads were not found. There were two female figures with prominent abdomens and broad hips, the marks of a pregnant woman. Such stone and clay

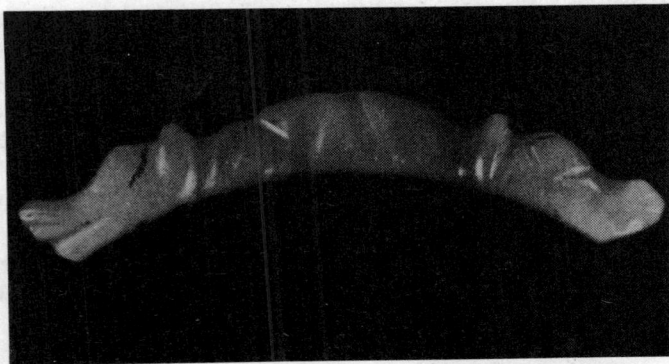

The double-dragon-head jade *huang* of the Hongshan Culture unearthed at Gezuo Dongshanzui, Liaoning Province

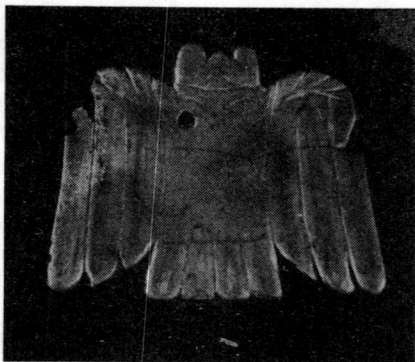

The owl shaped turquoise ornament

figures had been found in the remains of the Old Stone Age to the early Bronze Age at various regions of the world. They are regarded as the symbols of matriarchy, being the direct witness in ascertaining the matrilineal society. In our past Neolithic finds, similar details had been discovered not once or twice; witness of the Yangshao Culture coloured pottery vase shaped like a human mouth unearthed at Shaodian Dadiwan Site, Tai'an, Shandong Province; or the human mould with detectable sex characteristics on the coloured pottery vase unearthed at Liuwan, Sanpingtai, Qinghai Province. But those are only flat mould and decorations of wares. Only these two clay figures are like the stone sculpture unearthed in Europe; they are first such finds in China.

All of the Dongshanzui finds, particularly the female figures, must be closely connected with the stone building site. Experts are of the opinion that

The pottery woman figure
(front view)

The pottery woman figure
(side view)

since many stones stood in the square base but no traces of column bases nor column pits have been found, the building had no roof. It was likely a flat terrace with a sacrificial altar, and the female figures might have been the objects of a cult. The construction of the buildings is of a high level, symmetric and south-facing in accordance with old Chinese tradition. These are the most ancient religious remains of China yet discovered.

2. A Hongshan Culture jadeware tomb was

unearthed in the summer of 1973 at Hutougou, Fuxin County, Liaoning Province. The wares are animal images—a tortoise, an owl, a bird, a fish, etc. The jade tortoise is very true to life: head a little drawn in; eyes, beak and paws carve lined; hexagon designs on the back; a horizontal hole bored across the belly. The jade owl spreads its wings; its head and tail are finely lined; a transverse hole is drilled across the back. The carving of the bird is simple and neat, just about to take wing. Besides, there were also jade beads, rings, "*bi*", cloud-designed pendants, etc. The cloud pendant is milk white in colour, hollowed out in the middle, and has two holes on the upper rim.

The manufacture of these jade articles is quite unique, most of them only giving the outline of the creature without any additional adornment; they are accurate and symmetric. Holes were drilled transversely from two ends, which is a typical method of boring of the Neolithic Age.

3. The jade dragon of Sanxingtala, Wongniute Banner, Inner Mongolia, was discovered in 1971. It is dark green in colour, 26 centimetres high, with chin up, back arched, and tail curled. The mouth stretches forward, slightly up-turned and tightly shut. There are nostrils and a pair of protruding rhomboid eyes, a long mane over the neck, and a hole in the back. This is the largest jadeware of the Hongshan Culture.

The spot where the jade dragon was unearthed is a larger remain of the Hongshan Culture. From the same site, red clay pottery fragments pressed with "Z" designs have been collected. Compared with jade dragons of the Shang and Zhou dynasties, this is more original in appearance. The finds also provide new materials for the study of the origin of dragons in China and the ancient history of the Liaohe River Basin.

When Was the Earliest Chinese Ancient City Actually Built?
—On the Find of Shangcheng, Zhengzhou

Guo Bonan

Old Chinese cities are numerous; aside from Beijing, Nanjing, Luoyang, Xi'an, etc., there were Handan of the Zhao State, Linzi of the Qi State, Qufu of Lu, and Xianyang of Qin, all of which had a history of more than two thousand years. City walls and remains still survive today, and many cultural relics have been unearthed.

Older than these is the site of the remains of Fenggao, which was the founding capital of the Western Zhou Dynasty, situated at the southwest of Xi'an. There tombs of nobles have been discovered but the city proper hasn't been found yet.

The Zhouyuan Remains Site in Shaanxi Province is at the foot of the Qishan Mountains to the north, and by the side of Weihe River to the south. This was the birthplace of the ancient Zhou people, also known as the home of bronze. Several years ago a cluster of palaces of the Western Zhou Dynasty were found on the sites of Fengchu and Shaochen. Shell-and-bone record storage of the Western Zhou court was discovered, but here also, the remains of cities have not been found.

The Yin Dynasty site northwest of Anyang was the later capital of the Shang Dynasty for 273 years, where broadscaled ruins of palaces and even pottery drainpipes underground have been found. It is evident that this was a vestige of urban construction, but the city site has not yet been discovered.

But, after all, hadn't any city been built before the Shang Dynasty? This was a research problem which had been discussed for thirty years, commencing with the grave discovery at Zhengzhou, Henan Province.

The Mystery of the Old City

Henan Province is in the central region of ancient China, the centre of activity of the Chinese people for several thousand years, where archaeological relics are numerous above and beneath the ground. The old city of Zhengzhou with a circumference of 4.5 kilometres is the ancient site of the Qin and Han dynasties, at least two thousand or more years old. During the early stage of the founding of the People's Republic of China, a time of great building, the remains of pottery making were found to the west of Zhengzhou; to the north, a bone appliance workshop was discovered; and in the south, tombs and bronzes were unearthed.

Repeated finds show there are vestiges of ancient handicraft workshops around the old city, but where on earth was the city itself?

Soon after, the finds in the People's Park of Zhengzhou made a stir in the whole country. The ruins there are divided into two cultural strata. In the upper layer, implements unearthed are from the later period of the Shang Dynasty, the same as those from the Anyang Yin Dynasty ruins. Still more important are those relics from the lower stratum which have been determined to be from the early period of the Shang Dynasty. Viewed from the distinct point of cultural strata, these are the first such finds in archaeological history. So we can say that the suburbs of the old city cover a museum of the early stage of the Shang Dynasty, and that the finds in the park are the key of the exhibition hall. Owing to the finds of the Anyang Ruins scores of years ago, the acknowledged cultural history of China had been traced back several hundred years further. The present finds further enlarged our historic scope.

Nevertheless, when was the ancient city first constructed?

A Rammed-Soil Wall

In 1955, when unearthing the ancient city, the Henan working team excavated rammed-soil and pottery fragments in the depth. Because brick and tile baking had not been invented before the Western Zhou, the basic method of construction was with rammed soil. Even the refilled soil of graves was rammed in order to make it solid; therefore, once rammed soil appeared, the finds would be walls, a building base, or tombs. Pottery fragments are also the footprints of history. Judging from their shape, design and degree of baking, archaeologists can determine the phases of human culture of ten thousand years; there-fore, the archaeologists dug deeply on the spot to look for the fringe of rammed soil. Unexpectedly, however, they discovered a small grave of the early Shang Dynasty on the rammed-soil stratum.

Groping for the rim of the hardened soil of the "grave", they went scores of metres to the east and west; however, the rim still was not found. They unanimously believed that this was a rammed-soil wall of the early Shang Dynasty and wrote the discovery in *Archaeological Finds of New China*.

The soil wall is broad and long; isn't it the city wall of the ancient capital?

According to records, the early capital of the Shang Dynasty was Ao, located to the west of Zhengzhou at the foot of Mangshan Mountain in the district of ancient Yingzhen, but the site had not been found. Nevertheless, through years of groping, archaeologists have discovered that the hardened soil was just the wall of a square city—with three sides, the south, east and west, overlapping the ancient city of Zhengzhou. But the north side is far beyond the Qin and Han city wall. The square city has a 7 kilometre perimeter and a total area of 25 square kilometres, even larger than the Yin Ruins; it is identified as Shangcheng of Zhengzhou.

The city was built in 1620 B.C., and was not destroyed through the more than 3,500 years because it was in use a long time after the Shang Dynasty. It was repaired during the Warring States Period and further widened and heightened in the Han Dynasty. Well-preserved remnants of the city still measure 6 to 7 metres high and more than a score of metres wide at the base; experts estimate a million cubic metres of soil were needed to build the city.

Guo Moruo visited the spot and believed it might be the capital of Zhongding, the 11th King of the Shang, although records noted that his capital was "Ao". Other scholars thought that Shangcheng of Zhengzhou might be the ancient Xihao (West Hao), King Tang's capital; in any case, Shangcheng was the earliest king's city built in ancient China.

New Finds in the Ancient City

In the early seventies, rows of column pits of the rammed-soil foundation of a Shang palace were unearthed at the northeast corner of Shancheng. The foundation measured 60 metres long and nearly 10 metres wide. The column pits were orderly, lined 2 metres apart, one after another, with stones at the bottom of the pits. At the side of the wall base there was an abandoned ditch in which were heaped a hundred or more human skulls, each being sawed apart with distinct traces of the saw remaining.

To the west of Zhengzhou Shangcheng, two bronze quadripods have been unearthed. The smaller one is 87 centimetres high, and the bigger one is one metre high. Both are among the largest of the early Shang Dynasty bronzes, several hundred years earlier than the big tripod "Shimuwu" unearthed from the Yin Ruins. A tripod was the emblem of sovereignty in the slave system epoch. Palaces and quadripods further convinced archaeologists that Shangcheng was not an ordinary ancient city, but a kings' capital.

Through years of research, archaeologists realized

that the territory of the Shang Dynasty was not limited to the small lower reaches of the Yellow River, but that its culture had reached far to the north of the Great Wall and further to the district of Liaoning; and to the south of Yangtse River to the provinces of Guangxi and Hunan. In such a vast land, how many more ancient city sites can archaeologists expect to find?

In the beginning of the seventies, an eighty-thousand-square-metre ancient city was discovered 5 kilometres to the north of Wuhan, Hubei Province. "Panlongcheng" (the Coiled Dragon City) was established more than 3,500 years ago.

In 1983, at the west of Yanshicheng, Henan Province, an ancient Shang city was discovered. "Yanshi-shangcheng" covers an area of 1,900,000 square metres, and is the earliest Shang city known today. According to the geographic locus and historic documentation, this is one of the Shang capitals, "Xihao". If Xihao is at Yanshi, then Zhengzhou Shangcheng must be King Zhongding's Capital "Ao". Of course, this should be further verified.

The Beginning of An Urban Area

A city is the fruit of social productivity; from the layout of the Shangcheng Ruins, we can see that slave owners lived in the city while slaves laboured in workshops outside the city. Class society differences are distinctly partitioned by the construction of the great city wall. Therefore, it is quite necessary to find out the origin of an ancient city in order to understand the early civilization of China. From the enormous size of the project and the skillful ramming technique of Shangcheng, it was not a preliminary work but matured; there must have been a long history of city building.

The records say "Gun built a city" and "Yu made his capital at Yangcheng." In other words, the Chinese ancient city was built in the early stages of the Xia Dynasty or even before that time. Yangcheng is in Dengfeng County at the foot of the Songshan Mountains. Through years of investigation of the site, the rammed city wall foundation was discovered to be on a highland called "Wangchenggang" (the Mound of King's City). The building site, storing caves, ash pits, and fragments of stone, bone and bronze wares have been unearthed. The ancient city is more than four thousand years old, circa the beginning of the Xia.

Wangchenggang was part of Yangcheng before the Qin Dynasty, but has not been positively identified as the capital of Yu because the city is too small. It measures only 100 metres long on each side, more a castle than a city. Besides, no corresponding palaces and graves have been found on this spot. Also, at the ruins of the Erlitou Culture at west Henan and south Shanxi, a royal palace cluster and graves of burial jade and pottery wares have been discovered. Still, Wangchenggang is a remnant site of the Xia Dynasty, which is of great significance.

Another more important ancient city of China is at Pingliangtai, Huaiyang County, Henan Province. The city, which is part of the Longshan Culture, has a total area of 50,000 square metres and remnant walls more than three metres high. By the sides of the south city wall gate there were a pair of ushers' rooms built of adobe; under the city street there are pottery drainage pipelines which are important for studying the history of the construction of Chinese cities. From the scope of Pingliangtai, we can see the history of a city is not limited to four thousand years. But the problem which still arouses the interests of archaeologists is, "where are the earlier cities?"

Another Battalion of Pottery Men and Horses Came out from the Earth

Xin Qi

The ancient city of Xuzhou, to the northwest of Jiangsu Province, was the capital of the Chu State during the Western Han Dynasty. It is a strategic point, contested from olden times. In December 1984, while building workshops, construction workers discovered the burials of Prince Chu. To date, 2,500 men and horses have been excavated from a total of more than 4,000. This is another battalion of troops coming up to the world after the Xi'an finds in 1974.

Two infantry pits have been cleared out. Three strips of pits, each measuring 28 metres long, 2.5 metres wide and 60 centimetres deep, have been discovered. A cavalry pit was also found to the northwest of the above pits, measuring 12 metres long and 3 metres wide.

In the infantry pit, standing figurines were arranged 10 in a row, while sitting figurines were placed either 8, or 5 to 6 in a row. The moulded pottery is grey or brownish-grey in colour. After being baked, the whole body was whitened; some of the parts were painted with red pigments and the heads were blackened. Owing to the long and acidic burial, most of the colours faded; very few were retained. More than ten types of figures over 50 centimetres tall were made, including soldiers who were standing, kneeling, armoured, and mounted on horseback, and generals as well.

In front of the east end of No. 1 Pit there is a command cart pulled by four horses. The horses with their chins up, ears erect, and eyes glaring, still stand there. All the horses have heavy, rounded buttocks, strong legs, and knotted tails, and are vigourous and alert. On the cart stands a general, wearing a helmet and clad in a long robe, cupping his hands before his breast. There is a small hole in the hand, into which, it seems, was inserted the mark of command. There is also a hole under his left chest which seems to have been left by a decayed wooden sword. The general has the air of a veteran commander: a broad forehead, eyes looking afar, and mouth shut.

Armoured soldiers with quivers on their backs kneel on both knees. There is a larger number of standing figurines, some with banner and halberd; they seem to be honour guards. Some archers have their hands bent and quivers on their backs. Each is different from the others—their heads are helmeted, or hair is braided or coiled; facial expressions are solemn, quiet, broad-minded, or worried; eyes are widened or slightly closed, mouths opened or shut, noses flat or high, nostrils extended or shut. Among the figurines no one is bearded; they were all young and strong. In other words, the population of the Chu State was flourishing, and their manpower resources were abundant.

Through investigation, it has been discovered that the pottery figures belong to a certain prince of Chu in the middle age of the Han Dynasty. The tomb owner was enfeoffed at Xuzhou during the Western Han. The soldiers were his bodyguards. His tomb is most likely at a spot in the Lion Hillock, around two hundred metres to the east of the Pit, or in another nearby hillock; this remains to be discovered.

The unearthed figures reflect the battle formation of the Chu troops; they render important data to the study of Chu social customs, military equipment, constitution, handling, system and arm of services, etc. They also afford reference to the art of sculpture and the costume of the Han Dynasty.

The Museum of Xuzhou Pottery Figurines of the Han Dynasty has been opened at the site. The museum revealed that this batch of relics is only a part of the burials; more valuable treasures are likely to be excavated before long.

The Culture of the Ancient Dian State

Luo Yefen

The bronze culture of the Shang Dynasty (c. 16th —11th century B.C.) is the pride of the Chinese people, but few know the bronze culture of the ancient Dian State at Yunnan Province. The Dian State existed in the third century B.C. but faded away, together with its bronze culture, from the historic arena in the first century B.C. The social state, politics, economy, culture and customs of the Dian State could no longer be found in literary records. However, since the excavation of Dian tombs at Jinning Shizhaishan, Wangchuan Lijiashan, Anning Taijishan, Chuxiong Wanjiaba, etc., the unearthed relics have filled in the blanks.

One of the most significant relics is the 95 percent pure gold seal of the Prince of Dian, which clarified the political relations between the Western Han Dynasty (206 B.C.—8 A.D.) and the Dian State. *Records of the Historian* noted that Han Emperor Wudi granted a seal to the prince of Dian in the year 109 B.C. The find of the seal borewitness, not only to the fact that the regions of Yunnan belonged to the Dian State, but also to the fact that Yunnan had long been brought under the Han's domain.

From the large tomb burials were unearthed a massive display of wealth, with such items as bronze appliances, productive tools, sacrificial vessels, musical instruments, weapons, buckles, ornaments of jade, glass and turquoise, as well as a large amount of cowry money. This shows that the tomb owners were rich, a distinct contrast to the tombs of the common people.

As noted in *Records of the Historian*, during the 8th to 1st century B.C., Kunming and neighbouring tribes were braided people while the Dians were banded people. (The braided tribes wore their hair in braids, while the banded Dians tied their hair back in buns.) They were hostile to each other for a long period of time. On the Dian bronzes, the images of slaves are mostly braided people.

An unearthed Dian bronze shows two Dian warriors coming back from victory, carrying Kunming

Bronze teapoy composed of cattle and tiger

Bronze buckle ornament

men's heads in their hands. The dead men's wives and children are driven off to be their slaves, and cattle and herds become their booty. This tells us that slaves of the time were usually war captives. Other bronzes reflect scenes of slave killing for sacrifice. Such was the primitive, savage custom of the time.

A bronze reflects the spring sowing ceremony: four silverbanded Dian female slaveowners are carried on sedans by four male slaves each with rows of servants behind, carrying hoes and ploughs on their shoulders, and men and women carrying grain seeds on their heads. This ceremony is religious and sacrificial, as well as agricultural. Another bronze work shows the religious rite of pregnancy, held every year to welcome the autumn harvest, as the Dians held that crops are just like human beings—produced through pregnancy, birth and growth.

On the bronzes, farming, religious and social activities are all conducted by women, which implies that the farming economy of the ancient Dian still retained the matriarchal system.

The above mentioned farming activities and the unearthed bronze implements explain that the agricultural productivity had come to a certain scope.

From the bronzes, some 50 kinds of animal images could be found, including cattle, horses, sheep, pigs, snakes, peacocks, tigers, deer, leopards, etc., among which cattle and snakes are most numerous. At the time, cattle played an important role in the social economy and were the symbol of wealth; aside from slaves, cattle were the main sacrificial offerings and also the main source of meat. Ox fighting was an indispensable recreation of the Dians, but cattle never appeared in portraits of ploughing. Snakes were worshipped as gods in religious and sacrificial activities.

On a bronze plate there are carved braided slaves in fetters; head images of cattle, sheep, horses, tigers, leopards, etc.; wine vessels (representing wine); baskets (representing cereals); the head of a walking stick (representing power), as well as some spinning and weaving implements. Under each image is marked a different number of cowry, circle and dash marks; these might be the Dians' pictographic records of events, which are valuable in researching the etymology of minorities. It is very hard for this kind of character to describe the state, trend, time and location of events; therefore, a realistic style is the unique feature of the Dian bronze culture. Carved on the lids of bronze cowrie containers are such vivid scenes as warfare, sacrificial services, spinning, weaving, and paying tribute, etc., together with those reflecting grazing and dancing. All of these recorded the social life and customs of the Dians.

Cowries in the bronze container were used by the Dians for trading; appraisal shows that they came from both the Pacific and Atlantic oceans. Among the unearthed relics are glass and bronze cases, etc.: foreign imported objects which bear witness to the Dian's business relations on land and sea.

The large amount of relics of bronze, iron, gold, silver, jade, lacquer, pottery, leather, and textiles reflects the flourishing handicrafts of the Dian society. A piece of armour, its copper sheet as thin as one millimetre, is engraved with designs of a bear, leopard, deer, cock, pig, monkey, fish, lizard, bugs, and bees

Bronze cowry container

Bronze cowry container with the scene of sacrificial service on its lid

—meticulous, vivid and interesting—which marked the excellent technique of the Dian's bronze casting. Other bronzes reflect scenes of musical dancing, with as many as scores of dancers in a cluster, accompanied by a *sheng*, bronze drum, series bronze bells, gong, etc.

The bronze drum is a unique relic of the southwest minorities. The drum discovered at Wanjiaba was made in the 8th to 5th century B.C.; it is said that it is the earliest drum ever found in the world. The bronze drum was changed from a cooking utensil into a musical instrument, and further developed to be the token of wealth and power of the slaveowners.

The Dian bronze culture reached its climax in 221 B.C.; a little later Emperor Qin Shi Huang (221—210 B.C.) unified China. Standard post roads were built to the border of the Dian State, strengthening its relation with the Central Regions. During the Western Han Dynasty, Han Emperor Wudi extended his influence to the southwest; the advanced culture of the Han people came into contact with the Dian and hastened the economic development of the Yunnan slave society, while disintegrating the Dian slave society. Soon the ancient Dian State disappeared from the historic arena.

The Discovery of a Missing King's Tomb

Cao Bailong

Intent on looting the legendary tomb treasures of the King of Nanyue, Sun Quan (182-252 A.D.), a king of Wu during the Three Kingdoms period, ordered his troops into the area (in the vicinity of today's Guangdong Province and the Guangxi Zhuang Nationality Autonomous Region. They searched for the tomb to no avail. Who was to know that, like a fairy tale, the tomb would accidentally be discovered at Guangzhou over seventeen centuries later?

The Nanyue's King tomb is the largest stone-house tomb ever excavated, and has the greatest quantity of relics. All the Han tombs throughout the nation had been robbed before their excavation, but the Nanyue King's tomb had been kept intact over the past seventeen hundred years. Its scientific value can well keep pace with the Mancheng and Mawangdui tombs.

The Nanyue Kingdom

The Nanyue Kingdom was a separatist regime in today's Guangdong Province, during the early stages of the Western Han Dynasty. It was a short-lived kingdom, handed down through five generations over a period of ninety-three years. Very little has been written in Chinese books about the history of this kingdom; the new finds fill the gap in this respect.

The first king, Zhao Tuo, had been a Qin general stationed there to control the Yues. At the end of the Qin Dynasty when the whole nation was suffering from the chaos of war, he set up the local regime, calling himself the Warring King (Wuwang) of the Nanyue Kingdom. When Han Emperor Gaozu (206—195 B.C.) unified China, Zhao Tuo was made the Prince of Nanyue. Zhao Tuo lived to more than a hundred years of age, surviving all of his sons, and handed the throne to his grandson Zhao Hu (also known as Zhao Mei), called the Civil King (Wenwang) of Nanyue, who reigned for ten more years. The third king, Zhao Yingqi, was succeeded by Zhao Xing, then by Zhao Jiande. The last two kings died in warfare, and the kingdom was at last destroyed by Han Emperor Wudi (87—56 B.C.). The tomb owner could only be one of the first three kings, but the actual one still could not be identified at that time.

First Exploration of the Ground Palace

By early June 1983, a work unit was building a dormitory on the hillock of Xianggang (49.7 metres above sea level) at the west flank of Yuexiu Park. When the hilltop had been shoved down 17 metres, the bulldozer ran into a large piece of slabstone, on which appeared a break of 2 x 30 centimetres. A stone house grave was found under the slab.

Archaeologists rushed to the spot and saw numerous treasures in the grave: bronze pail, bronze flask, bronze "*fang*" (a large, full-bodied container), bronze tripod, full set of series bells, series cymbals and chimes. The walls of the front room are painted with black and coloured cloud designs; the east flank room holds large bronzes, including sets of series bells and chimes; in the west flank room are also stored bronze and jade wares. All the things have been appraised as belonging to the Kingdom of Nanyue of twenty-one centuries ago.

Tomb Owner Revealed

The news of the finds shook the archaeology world. The Excavation Team of the Xianggang Han Tomb was formed immediately by the Archaeology Institute of the Chinese Academy of Social Sciences, the Guangzhou Ancient Relics Management Committee and the Guangdong Provincial Museum, and formally started to excavate the tomb on August 25, 1983.

The tomb pit was made by levelling off the hilltop twenty metres deep into the ground into a 凸 -shaped longitudinal section. The whole tomb is 10.85 metres long from north to south and 12.43 metres wide from east to west. It is divided into a front room and east and west wing rooms; each room is sealed by double sets of stone gates. The top of the grave is covered by 24 large slabs of stone.

In front of the first stone gate along the path leading to the coffin chamber, there are large lumps of stone, weighing several hundred kilograms each, which were heaped there to hinder robbery. However, the first stone gate had toppled down already. Along the sides of the grave passage and in front of the front room there are a lot of pottery wares on which were inscribed "Changlegongqi" (ware of the Ever-Happy Palace) and affixed the king's seal before baking. This is evidence of a king's tomb, but still, who was he? His identity was still unknown.

The second stone gates lead to the main chamber. They are 1.8 metres high and 1.6 metres wide, weighing at least one ton; in spite of the passage of two thousand years, they were still tightly closed. The animal's head bronze knockers on the stone gates look formidable. There was an automatic device to hold the gates after closing. Below one of the gates, the excavators dug a channel into which they let the gate fall, then winched it up. In this way the gates were preserved and the burials left intact.

In the center of the chamber were placed the inner and outer coffins, which had totally decayed; only the remains were left. The tomb owner is clad in a jade shroud with ten swords round his waist; gold and jade adorn his head. Beside his head was placed a lacquer case full of pearls; in front of the chest were strings of beads made of gold, silver, jade, glass and pearls as well as pendants of a sculptured jade dragon and phoenix. Below the jade clothes were 30 more jade "*Bi*" as big as 30 centimetres in diameter; by the shoulders were placed a green jade animal-head *Bi* and other round and hollowed jade objects; all are meticulous and the best among Han wares.

There are six seals on the dead body, the greatest one is a golden dragon noded seal, square shaped — 3.1

centimetres long on each side and 1.8 centimetres high including the node, weighing 148.5 grams, and bearing 4 characters, "Wen Di Xing Xi" (The Civil King's Executing Seal)—this is the greatest golden seal of the Western Han Dynasty ever discovered. Another seal is "Zhao Mei Yin" (Zhao Mei's seal), which was unearthed together with the above-mentioned seal; therefore the tomb owner has been determined to be the second king of the Nanyue Kingdom. *Records of the Historian* wrote the name as Zhao Hu, which is a mistake. The finds not only identify the tomb owner but also correct the mistake of history books.

The Cruel Burial Sacrificial System

In six rooms there are more than ten burial skeletons; in the east wing room (where maids and concubines are buried) there were four concubines who were sacrificed while alive. The top right body has a gold seal while the other three have only gold-plated copper seals—because in the ancient lore the right-hand side is more respectable. In the same room, aside from the jade wares, there is a piece of flat transparent glass, 9.5 x 4.5 x 0.3 centimetres. It is light blue in colour and the same as modern glass. This is the earliest flat glass ever unearthed from tombs.

The western room was for cooks and servants; bones of sacrificial animals such as cattle, pigs, chickens, birds, fish and turtles have been found. There are seven sacrificial skeletons without any coffins at all who were thrown alive directly onto the wooden floor. Six are grown-ups, while a child clings to the bosom of one of the adults. Very few burial objects accompany them; it is quite possible they were servants.

In the Han tombs so far excavated, live sacrifice has never been found, whereas in the Nanyue Kingdom the ancient savage custom was still retained.

The Underground Museum

Most of the more than a thousand valuable relics were unearthed from the wing rooms. In the east flank are placed mainly musical instruments and wine vessels: a set of 14 bronze bells with knobs; two sets of stone chimes—18 pieces; a set of "yong" bells—5 pieces; a set of cymbals—8 pieces; and a batch of bronze "*tong*", tripods, "*fang*" and "*hu*" (pots), etc. In the west flank there are bronze sacrificial vessels; bronze and pottery daily appliances; bronze and iron weapons; armour, bows and arrow-heads; tools for making writing-slips; carts and curtains; jade and stone ornaments; gold, silver, ivory, lacquer, bamboo and wooden wares; silk clothes; medicines and stone needles of different colours; seals and clay stamps, etc., totalling more than 500 pieces. One of the pieces is a bronze mirror, 41.5 centimetres in diameter, with face and back separately cast. On the face is a lacquer-painted figure, and the back has beautiful carvings inlaid with turquoise. This is the biggest Han mirror ever excavated. There is also a set of jade swords of 43 pieces; some are double-sided and hollow-carved, but most are surface-carved dragon, tiger or phoenix designs. In the west flank there are also unprocessed whole tusks of ivory.

The iron sword worn by the grave owner is as long as 1.4 metres, the longest excavated from Han tombs; there are bronze crossbows and leaden bullets as well. A beautiful lamp was found, depicting three silver snakes holding a jade lamp in their mouths, crawling on a bronze plate; the like had never appeared before in Han tombs.

Behind the main room is a food storeroom. In a hundred bronze and pottery vessels are contained the remnants of bones and shells of land and marine animals; one of the pottery jars contains a hundred headless and footless little birds.

The bronzes in the tomb are not only great in number but also exquisite in make, which testifies that the bronze casting at the time had attained a high level. Parts of the burials have a local flavour of their own but most of them are similar to those of the central regions, which demonstrates that the Nanyue Kingdom at the time was closely in touch with the interior. For example, wearing the jade shroud was a Han custom for emperors and princes.

Judging from the ivory articles, silver wares, and the beads of glass, agate, crystal and other materials, it is quite possible that a part of them had been imported from central or south Asia. This reflects the fact that Guangzhou did a lot of trade with foreign countries; nevertheless, the Nanyue Kingdom had no coins of their own, so their transactions still remained at the barter stage.

The excavation of this ancient tomb has come to a halt. The responsible organ is going to build a site museum for the exhibition of those unearthed burials for the research of home and foreign scholars. Other problems are under archaeologists' further exploration, such as the location of the tomb of the first King, Zhao Tuo. It should be in the neighbourhood of the present tomb, but its location is still unknown as of now. Part of the relics are still under repair, restoration, and research. Fresh information is expected from these precious relics.

Precious Buddhist Relics Newly Unearthed at Lintong

An Keren

An imperial Buddhist shrine, a set of silver outer and golden inner coffins and the Flourishing Tang Dynasty's frescoes were found in May 1985, in the ruins of the Tang-built Qingshan Monastery in Lintong County, Shaanxi Province. The site of the monastery is 4 kilometres to the northeast of the Qin pottery men and horses, and 40 kilometres from the ancient city of Xi'an. History books noted that Qingshan Monastery was one of the 48 monasteries built in the Sui and Tang dynasties. Under the basement of a pagoda, in a Buddhist Fine Room, an 82 centimetre-high monument was unearthed. The 500-word inscription narrated the story of this Imperial Buddhist Shrine, saying that the monastery had been blown down by a strong wind. The abbot of Wenguo Monastery, Chang'an, supervised the rebuilding of the monastery, but the pagoda was built by Abbot Da De Hui Deng of the monastery. The date of completion was the year 741.

For several months, archaeologists cleared the excavation site and studied the finds. The Fine Room is facing the south forming a " 甲 "-shaped flat section; outside the main room is a stone gate, with a finely linear- and relief-sculptured lintel and threshold. Inside the gate, in the middle of the main room is the square pavilion-shaped Buddhist Shrine, sculptured of green stone, 109 centimetres high. On the front, eight characters "Shi Jia Ru Lai She Li Bao Zhang" (Buddha's Shrine) were carved and gold-smeared. The pavilion has a peach-like pointed top; on each of the four corners of the lapped eaves stands a gold-filled phoenix, head up and taking wing. Gold-filled metals in ancient artifacts are not too rare, but gold-filled stone is a new find. Below the eaves are carved peony flowers and various kinds of flying Apsaras—some are scattering flowers down to the lower world; some are cupping fruits in their hands; some are blowing *sengs* (wind pipes clustering together to a mouthpiece) and others are plucking pipa lutes. Some of the flying nymphs have bodies of a phoenix, the artistic style of which is different from that of the Dunhuang Caves. They all are lively and vivid; they are excellent linear carvings of the Tang Dynasty. On the walls of the pagoda are Buddhist stories. The finding of the square pavilion-shaped stone shrine is indeed first in this country.

The cinerarium is hollow and contains a gold-filled bronze stand on which is a silver outer coffin, 21 centimetres long, 12 centimetres (broader end) to 7 centimetres (smaller end) wide, and 14.5 centimetres (broader end) to 10 centimetres (smaller end) high. Pearls, agate, crystal, jadeite, cat's-eye, etc., are inlaid on the lid, around which are tassels of stringed pearls. On the broader end is a gold-filled relief of Bodhisattva; on the smaller end, firing pearls; the two sides have 5 gold-filled arhats each. Below the outer coffin is the gold-filled copper "Xumi Mountain" stand—23.4 centimetres long, 17 centimetres wide and 12 centimetres high. Inside the outer coffin is a golden coffin, 14 centimetres long, 7.4 centimetres to 4.5 centimetres wide, 9.5 centimetres to 6.5 centimetres high. The coffin is encircled twice with silk threads; around the coffin are relief sculptured lions and inlaid purple and white gems and pearls; the whole coffin is solidly riveted. In the gold coffin is a green glass bottle which contains the crystal imitation of Buddha's burnt bone remains.

Beside the stone-sculptured shrine there are placed a hundred-odd sacrificial articles made of gold, silver, copper, pottery and glass; among them, the most precious are the two stems of golden lotus flowers. The pistils are made of green gems, surrounded with a circle of pearls; the leaf veins are meticulous; the whole thing was precisely wrought. In the tri-coloured plate before the shrine is a tri-coloured pottery pumpkin. This is the earliest find of pottery foodstuff of this kind. In the plates at two sides are bundles of green, brownish-yellow glass cones, 2 centimetres in diameter, with very thin and highly transparent walls; the skill with which they were made astonishes people today. These are profound practical objects for the research of our glass making in ancient times.

Beyond the stone gate are a pair of tri-coloured pottery lions of unique moulding; the left one, 16.2 centimetres tall, turns back to bite his hind leg; the right one, 17 centimetres tall, stands with hind legs protruding forward and scratches his itches with eyes shut. These two lions' bearing looks very funny; they are precious make of their kind indeed!

Among the sacrificial articles, the copper human-faced pot has a phoenix-headed slender neck and a phoenix-tailed handle; there are 6 faces in relief on the belly, 2 under one common braid; they have deep eyes and prominent pointed noses—typical of a Hindu type. Such novelties had never been found before; they are significant in the research of the cultural exchange with foreign countries in ancient times.

Other sacrificial articles include the following: a gold-filled incense burner, which can be set or hung, with feet and chains composed of 12 tiger heads and 6 tiger legs, a rare relic; a high-stemmed gold-filled cup, 6 centimetres tall, the fine make of which exhibits the high level of metal technology of the high time of the Tang Dynasty; silver spoons, chopsticks and copper alms bowls which still glitter today, though very few ordinary utensils have been unearthed; scores of white and black pottery bowls, dishes, plates, alms bowls, etc., which viewed from the completeness of preservation, are also first finds, offering material objects for studying kiln baking in ancient times.

On the three sides (east, west and north) of the seamless brick walls of the paved pass and the main hall are frescoes of Chinese and foreign monks, performances of singers and dancers, Buddha's warrior attendants, guards of prowess, etc. The lines of the paintings are graceful, the images vivid, the colouring bright; they are exceedingly precious paintings retained ever since the flourishing period of the Tang Dynasty.

The Mystery of the Guge Kingdom of Tibet

Tong Mingkang

Tibet is the roof of the earth, and the Ali District is the ridge of the roof. The district is the most deserted and secluded west frontier of China, the nearest to the sky, having Holy land, mountains, lakes and waters for Buddhist disciples to pay their homage. It is mysterious not only because it has many famous mountains, but also because more than a thousand years ago on the topmost plateau there was a "Celestial Kingdom" which vanished abruptly some three hundred years ago. That was the Guge Kingdom, the ruins of which are in Zada County of the Ali District.

In June 1985, an investigative team of 11 young people, average age below 30, was formed by the Tibet Cultural Relics Administration, Cultural Relics Press, the Palace Museum and Sichuan University; a team of young people was chosen to celebrate the year of International Youth. We bade farewell to Lhasa, to Zegyang, to Xigaze, and set forth along the line towards the site of the ancient Guge Kingdom.

The District of Ali has a vast land of 550,000 square kilometres, but a very small population, less than one per 10 square kilometres. Usually not a person was met on the way in a day. Between posts is at least a day's journey, and most posts do not afford provisions. Every morning we would have some solid food at random before setting forth. In order to eat, one must have water. Yes, on the way, we saw lakes of water everywhere, but that was salt water. It would be our good luck if we could melt some snow water to go with *zanba* (glutinous rice) and dried meat. Before leaving the spot, we would refill the "heaven dew" as full as the vessels could contain, because we were not sure whether there would be any snow ahead on the day's journey. That day when we started from Lazi we had no time for our breakfast. On the more difficult road we encountered no man and no water; everyone was thirsty and hungry, and some even had stom-achaches to a great extent. When we came to the 21st Post, it was already about 10 o'clock at night. The Post is 5,200 metres above sea level and has only one well, where the water was frozen. We broke the ice and fetched some water to cook our supper (On the plateau, the air is thin; cooked food is generally half-done). When we ate our food, it was already midnight. It is very cold there; the average year-round temperature is -6°C, and four seasons all of the whole year are winter. This was in mid-June, yet we shivered with cold. We made a bonfire with the faggots we had brought along in the car and sat around it; some even danced for warmth. When slightly warmed up, we began to go to bed. Two short hours had passed.

Ali District has a three-hour time difference from Beijing. Daybreak in June is at 8 a.m. and pitch dusk at 11 p.m. We were on the road 15 hours a day with two-hour stops for snacks; were we in Beijing, driving

13 hours at 60 kilometre speed, we would have travelled 800 kilometres a day—but that is impossible on the highland of Tibet. Amidst the mountains, the oxygen supply in the air is only 57 percent that of Beijing and the boiling point of water is only 80°C. All of these bring tremendous difficulties to travellers. Climbing on the precipitous road we had to repeatedly stop for rests; moreover, the road is rugged and rough, as a hollow pit in the road might contain a yak; sometimes we had to come down to push the car. Actually we could only travel two to three hundred kilometres a day. During our travels, we often thought of the hardships our PLA men and the natives of Tibet had endured in building the road which opened to traffic in 1957. Not a few lost their lives and were buried by the roadside with only the names and dates marked on a piece of stone. We couldn't help extending our heartfelt tribute to them. Were it not for their blood and flesh, the vast mountains would still be inaccessible today!

In the parts of Coqen and Gerze, the "No Man's" plateau of the north Tibet has an area of 200,000 square kilometres, as large as two Zhejiang provinces. By 6 p.m., we came to a silent, beautiful salty lake, the shore of which was formed by 15 metres wide white salt crystals. When our car was driven on the shore it began to sink into the mud; the more the driver thrust the deeper it sank. It was still as death, with no sign of man; in the tranquility we felt a kind of terror. The place was a vast natural zoo of wild beasts: deer, antelopes, yellow gazelles, wild yaks, wild horses, wild asses, wolves.... How many adventurers had lost their lives in this vicinity! We kept silent, carried levers and

47

went into the mud. Several hours passed and several bars were broken before we lifted up our car. We didn't cheer nor dance for joy, but hastened away from the place of death in the pitch dark night.

It was in the end of April, 1985, that we came to Lhasa at the request of the Tibet Cultural Relics Administration, to get a grasp of the history, religion, architecture and the ancient relics of the province. But a thorough understanding of the culture of the Ali District has, in a certain sense, still eluded our grasp.

We were proud of our investigation. Through all kinds of hardship, our predecessors had only brought back some unsuccessful photos of the ruins of the District, while our visit brought back much more detailed reports and video tape records.

On June 30th we entered the endless, steep gorge. The mountains are yellow in colour and totally barren; through ages, rocks have been weathered into the shapes of a castle, a palace, a pagoda and a Buddha Hall which are very fascinating. It is as if we were travelling amongst the largest ancient ruins of the world; what marvellous phenomena created by nature!

The wind blew and sand blotted out the sky and the earth; they were casting coloured paper scraps to receive our arrival.

Along the Xiangquan (Elephant Stream) River towards the west, through ranges of mountains, we came to a small hill. We could not help shedding tears. This was the end of our 17 days journey! This is a mound of rocks covered by a thick layer of yellow dust; the whole thing looks like a huge bee comb afflicted with all sorts of lesions. Such is the major nationally-protected historical relic nominated in 1961 as the ruins of the Guge Kingdom. At first sight, we were dumbfounded by the grandeur of its arrangement. But this is only a part of the ruins—the castle of the Kingdom. Half a kilometre to the east is another big castle; 5 kilometres away is a cluster of scores of caves. A kilometre to the northeast is the remain of a monastery—Zaburang; 40 kilometres further to the northeast is Zada County. There are several monasteries on the way, among which Tuolin Monastery is most famous. About 1.5 kilometres to the north is the Dried Corpse Cave, in which neighbourhood are military houses and remains of caves; 5 kilometres from here on the north bank of the Xiangquan River there are also scores of caves. Forty more kilometres to the southwest at Duoxiang is another large-scale ruin which, judging from the style of the construction of the rooms and caves, belongs to the remains of the Guge Kingdom. This is the largest ancient remain in Tibet.

The said castle is 200 metres high and covers an area of 200,000 square metres; there are 400 rooms and 800 caves at its east and south sides. The castle is divided into 11 storeys, comprising palaces monastic architectures, private residences and military installations; we made a full survey of them.

Palatial houses are on the hilltop, some with 40 rooms; most are one-storeyed, with a few two- or three-storeyed; the windows of higher buildings are still visible. The king and his family's rooms, which are small and exquisite, are on the east side of the south part of the hilltop; to the west of it are the ruins of a big hall covering some 200 square metres, which must have been a conference hall of the royal court. I am sure it was not a democratic spot, but a symbol of autocracy. In the north part of the hilltop there is an entrance leading to a cave. The path is rather steep; the first time we took it, we rolled down to the bottom where it suddenly became light. In the middle, there was a passage, by each side of which are four caves; the eastern four are pitch-dark in the belly of the hill, but the western four caves have windows on the cliff. Each cave is about 20 square metres large with a flat roof and steep walls; how nicely chiselled they had been! Here was the winter palace of the king. The whole palatial area was surrounded by adobe walls. The only passage from the belly to the top of the hill is a narrow, steep tunnel more than 50 metres long; intruders would have found it hard to enter.

Folktales say that during the reign of King Gesaer, Tibet was attacked by evil spirits which transformed themselves into a windstorm. Shelters blew away, herds died out and the population decreased day by day. The king was a hero on the battlefield but could not help with the tempest. One day, there came seven identical brothers; they dug the earth, felled trees, chiselled the rocky hill, and built the giant palace in a night. Immediately houses were built in the tempest rookeries of all Tibet. Since then, the people have been free of the threat of the windstorm. Knowing this, the god summoned the seven brothers to heaven to build houses for him, hence the "Northern Seven Brothers Stars" —*Qiang Ga Ben Dun* in the Tibetan dialect. In the Guge Ruins there are frescoes reflecting this story —long lumber-conveying teams were trudging along towards Guge....

There still exist six monasteries, two on the top and four at the foot of the hill. Each has its own characteristics; the White Temple and the Red Temple are the most splendid: each has an area of more than 300 square metres, typical of Tibetan style and still well-preserved after several hundred years. Beautiful frescoes are on the four walls, and all the ceilings are decorated with various designs. Standing in the temple, one seems to be visiting a magnificent gallery of art. The frescoes have a dense air of religion: there are life stories of Sakyamuni, devas of pleasure, and portraits of many other Buddhist stories as well as royal homage-paying to Buddha. On the ceilings of the White Temple there is a Buddha in the middle among the designs of every room; in short, the whole history of the Guge Kingdom has much to do with Buddhism.

Tibetans had their own native religion; Songtsan Gambo converted the kingdom into Buddhists and thereupon prospered. In 841, his son Langdama destroyed all the Buddhist temples and drowned, burnt or buried all the scriptures; the noted Dazhaoshi Temple became a slaughterhouse. That historic incident was called "Langdama's Buddhist Extermination", which closed the "Fore Prosperity Period" in the Buddhist history of Tibet. Langdama's grandson Chigidelimagong ran away to Ali and became king of Ali; his three sons each ruled a part of Ali and his third son, Dezhugong, became the first king of Guge during the upper decades of the tenth century. Dezhugong's eldest son Kere was a devoted Buddhist and became a monk called Zhiguang. During his son Lade's reign, he invited many learned monks to translate scriptures; among the monks, Renqingrangbo (Baoxian) was the most famous. He was born in Niangwangrenadu Village of the Guge district, visited India, studied Buddhism with

51

75 teachers, translated a large amount of scriptures and was a peerless master of the Later Prosperity Period. However, it was generally believed that the flourishing period began with the arrival of the learned monk Adisan from Bengal. A lot of valuable relics are still scattered in the present ruins of Guge—like the small clay (*caza*) and stone (*manishi*) Buddhas. From the frescoes we can see the real life of the time: scenes of sacrificial and celebrating activities, weapons and carts, palaces and houses, merry pastimes and acrobatics, etc.

What astonished us were the figures in the mural painting. Altogether thousands of them, all are lively and very few are identical. The ceiling designs have 500 kinds of exquisite composition; some of them are geometric or animal patterns, with 40 types of lion patterns alone. The brilliant colouring, dense and light, is in sharp contrast, mixing the styles of China's Interior, India, Nepal, and even West Asia; specialists call it "the Guge School". Standing before the painting, we are strongly amazed that illusive religious portraits seem to be our real life.

In the White Temple there are 20 clay sculptures, most of which had been broken; together with the wall paintings, we had them colour-video-recorded for later reproduction.

Also worth mentioning are two pagodas, both about 5 metres tall; the round based one is a god-descending pagoda (Laboquideng) and the square based one is called longevity pagoda (Langjiequideng). Both are unique in appearance, after the styles of India and Nepal. In the vicinity of Zaburang Monastery there are walls made up by 104 pagodas closely connected one by one. Magnificent work indeed!

During the investigation we discovered two mural-painted caves, three granaries, a mural burial and an armoury. The mural burial is in the First District Y103; it is a 4-roomed cave halfway up the hill with the mouth of the cave facing north. The central room is about 20 square metres; behind the other three sides are three rooms, each measuring 8 square metres. The western room is a granary, as evidenced by 10 centimetres thick highland barley on the ground, decayed. Along the north lower part of the east wall of the southern room is a big rock. When it was removed, we saw a niche on the wall, in which lies a withered little child, wrapped in coarse cloth, with a bracelet on his wrist. Under the little body are salt and green barley. To cast these two things into a grave is the custom of Tibet, from which we infer that mural burial is also a system of burial. In Tibet, as I understand, there are burials of earth, sky, fire, and water; but the mural burial is a first find throughout China.

One and a half kilometres north from the castle on the fault of the cliff there is a "Dried Corpse Cave", facing east and 2 metres up from the ground. In the cave are 3 rooms; the mouth of the southern room is only 20 centimetres high, so the interior of the room is unknown. The central room has an area of 10 square metres; the western room is about 5 square metres. Two or three layers of dead bodies are placed in these two rooms, with the head and body mostly separated; one of the whole corpses is bound, hands across the belly and legs bent. The turquoise hairpin and finger ring still look new, and the clothes are stained with blood. But, how do we explain this mysterious cavern?

Guge was a militant country; the God of War was painted everywhere to protect the people against invaders. In the ruins there are tunnels, blockhouses, and city walls. The tunnels are intricate and extend in all directions. The newly discovered armoury is a cavern on the hilltop. It has three rooms, with the entrance facing north; shields are kept in the southern room while arrows are in the central and western rooms. There is a tunnel at the east end of the cave, which leads downhill. In case of war, troops might be reinforced to the front through this tunnel. In the Guge Ruins, helmets, armour, horse armour, shields, arrows, arrowheads, etc., are scattered everywhere. The helmets are made from cow-hide and strung small iron scales which seem to have been silver plated; there are some 50 varieties of them. The shields are made from rattan strips, adorned with copper, and painted with red and black designs. Arrows are made from bamboo and some from wood; some of the arrows had been feathered, but most are semi-finished products. Arrowheads are made of iron; there are 15 varieties of them. From these relics we can see the military force of the Guge Kingdom, which must have won many battles. Maybe the Dried Corpse Cave was for the captives, because the Guge people would not have them exposed in the wilderness. From the standpoint of religious rites, the Guges would never make any funeral ceremony for the enemy, but just throw them into the cave. For their own criminals, there are two huge caves, one for men, the other for women; numerous bones of the dead are in the separate caves.

The Kingdom of Guge had been sustained for 27 generations from Dezhugong to Zhidimai; it was said, at high tide, its population was up to a hundred thousand. In the present ruins there are about 800 caves, each comprising one to four rooms of 10 square metres; there are also 400 houses of different sizes. Judging from these, the inhabitants of the castle at the time would not have exceeded ten thousand; added with inhabitants of the other ruins, they could not have exceeded twenty thousand. Today, the population of this spot is much less than that. Geologists have told us that within the last thousand years, the geographic environment and the bad climate of this region have not changed at all. To sustain such a big kingdom for so many years was indeed a miracle.

In Tibetan history, Guge and Tubo are always equally mentioned, not only because Guge had brought in the Buddhist religion but also because the Guge kings are the direct offspring of Songtsan Gambo.

The Guge Kingdom was destroyed by the Ladakes who lived 500 kilometres off in present Kashmir. They were brothers of the same lineage but fought for many years. The last battle was fought at Guge in the mid-17th century when the Manchus captured Beijing and demolished the Great Ming Empire. The Ladakes overthrew the Guge Kingdom but did not occupy that piece of land. To prevent the Guges' return, the Ladakes destroyed the castle. But temples were not destroyed because the Ladakes also believed in the Buddhist religion. Following the collapse of the kingdom, the Guges disappeared from the world. People say two hundred of them escaped from the massacre in the castle, but where did they go? In a small village some scores of kilometres off from the ruins, some of the inhabitants alleged that they are the Guges. We can't tell whether it is true.

Three hundred years have elapsed, yet the ruins of the Guge Kingdom are still lying there silent. Upon our visit, she seems to have a lot to tell us: her past glory and her bitter life. Guge is an unsolved puzzle and an unlifted buried treasure. As a kingdom, she had gone to heaven; as an ancient site, she is still a mystery. I invite the interested parties of the world to make her a visit.

Reviewing the Bronzes in the Exhibition of the Unearthed Rare Relics

Li Xueqin

The Palace Museum of Beijing celebrated the 35th anniversary of the founding of the People's Republic in the autumn of 1984 with the Exhibition of the Unearthed Rare Relics. The best of the new finds nationwide were put on display; the bronzes were a splendid portion of the exhibits. Some representative examples of the exhibits are described below.

The bone-handled knife is one of the earliest bronze objects, excavated from Weijiatai, Linxia County, Gansu Province. In recent years, Chinese archaeologists have probed the origin of Chinese bronze wares and found a series of objects from the sites of the New Stone Age. They are made of pure copper, bronze or brass. The said knife belongs to the Qijia Culture, during which period stone and bronze were simultaneously employed; objects were first found in 1924 at Qijiaping, Guanghe County, Gansu Province, hence the name of the culture. A bronze edge was sandwiched within the bone handle; judging from this, some of the smaller blades of the Qijia Culture might also have been sandwiched within bone or wood. At that time, craftsmen were unable to make larger articles.

Thirteen early Shang bronzes were found in the southeast corner outside the Shangcheng Site, Zhengzhou, Henan Province in 1982. Examples include a huge quadripod which is 81 centimetres tall, a rare article, and a wine vessel (*you*) with *taotie* (ogre-mask) designs. It is 50 centimetres high, with *kui* (dragon) medallions on the lid, snake-shaped ends on the loop handle, and a *taotie*-decorated belly. As we know, previously-found objects were all tape designed, but this *you* is fully decorated with flowers.

Early Shang bronzes have also been found in the west part of Liaoning Province. An awl-footed, deep-bellied round tripod was discovered in the Chaoyang District. The tripod from Kezuo Xiaobotaigou is an earlier bronze, 86 centimetres high, with a *taotie* tape-design below the rim of the mouth; its feet are nearly awl-shaped. Another batch from a tomb at Liujiahe, Pinggu County, Beijing, unearthed in 1977, is of the same age; a spice container (*he*) with a sealed mouth is on display.

There are many later Shang wares on exhibition. The most attractive is the Qin Zi square tripod, excavated in 1981 from Qucun Village, Quwù County, Shanxi Province; it is 25.5 centimetres high, with *kui* tape medallions below the rim of the mouth and a *taotie* design at the belly. It is inscribed inside at two ends with 29 characters. The maker's name was Qin Zi; Qin is an official title which is often seen on Shang bronzes. The form of numbering the years is the same as that on the shell and bones of the Shang Dynasty; the inscription showed that the last three kings had reigned for 20 years.

Later Shang wares have been found in many spots in China, each with its own regional features. From the north comes the *taotie*-decorated sacrificial stool (*zu*), excavated from Huaerlou, Yixian County, Liaoning Province in 1979; it is 14.3 centimetres high and 33.6 centimetres long. There are two bells hung under the base, a quite unique style. Those from the south are meticulous, such as the owl-shaped wine vessel (*you*) from Yingcheng County, Hubei, and another similar piece from Luoshan, Henan. The pig-shaped wine vessel (*zun*) from Xiangtan, Hunan, is 40 centimetres in height, 72 centimetres in length, and true to life in modelling.

The battle-axe with seven holes (*qiong yue*) from Panjialiang, Niezhong County, Qinghai Province, and the human face ornament from Dahuazhongzhuang, Nieyuan County, both belong to the Kayue Culture of the period between the Shang and Zhou dynasties. In the *Xi Qing Gu Jian* there is an axe of the same shape which had not been dated; judging from the recently unearthed objects, they must have been wrought by an ancient minority. The many facial types depicted on the face-ornament are of value in researching the images of the ancient local people.

Among the early Zhou bronzes, meticulous works from Zuyuangou of Baoji and Zhuangbai of Fufeng in Shaanxi Province have been known to the world. Small feet have been attached to the *zun* and *you* from Zuyuangou, a make which is new to us. The Shiqiang plate from Zhuangbai is still as bright as new, with a long inscription telling the early historical events of the Zhou Dynasties. These are unrivalled treasures.

An inscription of particular significance is on the

quadripod of Marquis Teng from the tomb of Zhuang-lixicun, Tengxian County, Shandong Province, excavated in 1982. It is 27 centimetres high with a *kui*-shaped flat node on the lid, and has ears, *taotie* designs around the rim of the mouth, a *taotie*-adorned belly and four feet. It is an early Zhou ware. The inscription proves that the fief of Teng is at the present Tengxian County; the ancient records are accurate.

The unique modelling of the bird-lid pot (*hu*) and the mandarin wine vessel (*zun*) from Muzidun, Dan-tu, Jiangsu Province, attracts visitors' attention. This group of bronzes belongs to the early period of the Western Zhou Dynasty—the Wuyue Culture. In the 1950's, the cereal container (*jiu*) of Marquis Yi (Yi Hou Shi Jiu) and other important objects were unearthed from a mound grave not far from Muzidun. Archaeologists determined that they are from the same origin—the State of Wu.

The later period cooking tripod *li* and *gui* of the Western Zhou Dynasty excavated from Wangcun Village, Ningxian County, Gansu Province, are both inscribed. No bronze had been found on this spot in the past; it is at the east end of Gansu Province but not in the frontier of the country. Later Shang wares now on show were all excavated from Chongxin and Jingchuan, which are not far from Ningxian. To the north of these spots, from Sunjiazhuang, Guyuan, Ningxian, Western Zhou tripods and *gui*s have also been found in tombs. But very few bronzes of this period had been found in Ningxian in the past.

Among the exhibits there are several groups of noted bronzes of the Spring and Autumn Period. From a co-burial of the prince and his spouse of the Huang

Princedom, excavated in 1982 in Baoxiangshi, Guangshan, Henan Province, come "Huang Fu Ren Hu" (Madame Huang's pot), full of local taste. It is a precious artifact indeed, with a design of curled dragons sticking out their tongues. An inscription is on the outer wall, and the surface of the pot is as bright as new, without any rust.

The animal-head tripod from Yangjiapai, Huaining County, Anhui Province, is of the same make as those from Shucheng and other neighbouring spots; they probably represent the culture of the ancient Shu. The dragon-eared *zun* (wine vessel) from Wangcun, Qingyang County, Anhui Province, found in 1979, is similar to those two reproduced at the Shanghai Museum, and helps to identify the date of the reproductions.

Still more important is the bronze group from Xiashi, Xichuan County, Henan Province. Its date, most scholars opine, is of the later middle age of the Spring and Autumn Period, but others place it in the earlier late age of the Period. The Wang Zi Wu tripod on exhibit was made by Zigeng, the premier of the Chu State, which fact had been noted in *Zuo's Spring and Autumn Annals*; the finding of the bronze proves that the *Annals* is a reliable historical book, as the name and official position are same as the inscription on the bronze. Another exhibit is the inscribed bronze plate (Prince Xu, Yichu's plate) excavated in 1979 from Xingshan, Jing'an County, Jiangxi Province; the name Xu Yichu had been noted in *Zuo's Annals*.

The footed plate (*jin*) from Xiashi, Xichuan, Henan Province, is 28 centimetres high, 107 centimetres long, and meticulously adorned with hollowed-out cloud designs; there are 12 tiger-shaped adornments on the four walls and 10 tiger feet under the plate, a fanciful conception; this large and fine piece of bronze represents the high level of the Chu's bronze making in the Spring and Autumn Period.

The bronzes from the No. 1 Tomb, Hougudui, Gushi County, Henan Province, have also been put on display. A set of series bells (*bo*) had each been inscribed, but the owner's name had been wiped out; there must have been some complications in the matter.

Another worth mentioning is the King of Wu, Fucha's spear (*mao*) which was found in 1983 at Mashan, Jiangling, Hubei Province. The King of Wu, Fucha was conspicuous in the end years of the Spring and Autumn Period; his implements had been repeatedly discovered but this spear is a first. At the time, Wu's weapons were famous; this spear justifies that renown.

Among the bronzes of the Warring States we have to mention the batch excavated in 1982 from Potang, Shaoxing, Zhejiang: of great historical interest is a tripod of the Xu State which must have been brought back to Yue State as booty after their conquest of the Wu State, which traded with the Xu. However, still more interesting is the bronze house from the same batch: the house is comprised of three rooms; the front is open with pillars, and there are windows on the back. There are six men sitting in the room, playing the zither (*qin*), blowing the pipe organ (*sheng*), and beating the drum while over the top a bird sits on a pole. This bronze reflects the actual life of the ancient Yue people.

The tripods, dagger-axe (*ge*) and implements unearthed in 1980 from a big tomb of Jiuliandun, Xindu, Sichuan, belong to the Bashu Culture of the earlier middle age of the Warring States period. When excavated, the bronzes are bright as new; even the attached ropes and wooden handles are still well preserved, a miracle indeed. The wares are full of unique Bashu character inscriptions.

Those mentioned above were unearthed from the south of China. The gold-inlaid silver pot (*hu*) from Nanyaozhuang, Yuyi, Jiangsu, though unearthed in the south, is a Yan ware, as has been confirmed by its inscription. The pot is adorned with splendid stereo penta-petal flowers, and the artistry is in no way inferior to the south. The dagger-axe (*ge*) from Wulihe, Lingyuan, Liaoning Province, has black cloud designs and is also a Yan ware.

The hunting-designed stemmed bowl (*dou*) found in Sanji, Pingshan, Hebei Province in 1978, has a lid and small ring ears; judging from its age and location, it must be a bronze of the Zhongshan Kingdom. Its design has the characteristics of the northern style.

Bronzes of the Qin and Han dynasties on exhibit are also prominent.

In 1978-80, at Wuotuocun, Zibo, Shandong Province, five implement pits of Prince Qi's Tomb of the Western Han Dynasty were excavated. Among the wares, the bronze dagger-axe has a golden handle-covering (*bimao*) and the gold *zun* (wine vessel) is also very exquisite; both wares must have belonged to the prince himself. The huge rectangular mirror is 115.1 centimetres long, 57.7 centimetres wide, and 56.5 kilograms in weight, surrounded with are designs, adorned with *chi* (dragon) designs on the back and attached with five knobs. It is an unparalleled discovery of the ancient mirrors—the acme of perfection.

Unearthed articles from the tomb of kings of Nanyue are also exhibited. Some of their makes are unusual and grotesque: lamps are made into the shapes of dragons, birds and fantastic animal heads. A set of series-cymbals in eight pieces is inscribed "The Ninth Year of Wendi, made by the Imperial Conservatory". Wendi is the title of Nanyue's second king's reign, corresponding to Yuanguang 6th year of Han Emperor Wudi's reign (129 B.C.). The restored frame of the cymbals is set there as it was in the Shang Dynasty (5 cymbals from Fuhao Tomb of the Yin Dynasty ruins).

Another precious find from the Nanyue Tomb is the six-*shan* (mountains) back designed mirror; as we know, 4-*shan* designed mirrors are common, but 3-, 5- or 6-*shan* designed are rare. Six-*shan* mirrors had previously been recorded but none of them had been excavated. This is the only one accurately dated and sited.

Several bronze horses are on display: the pair from Fanglingcun, Xushui, Hebei, is strong and vigorous, yet they do not rival the huge horse from Fengliuling, Guixian, Guangxi. Together with the horse there was a groom figure. All of these horses belong to the Eastern Han Dynasty. Another gold gilded bronze horse excavated from Maoling, Shaanxi, looks sumptuous and brilliant, the best of steeds.

The bronzes above mentioned from the tomb of Prince Ji and the King of Nanyue all belong to the princedom class, while those from the No. 1 pit of Maoling (Han Emperor Wudi's Tomb) are of the emperor class, of course more gorgeous than any others. Among the exhibits, the bamboo-joints incense burner (*xun lu*) had been inscribed with *Yang Xin jia* (belonging to the Elder Princess Yangxin,) the elder sister of Han Emperor Wudi). The Changxin Palace lamp from the tomb of Zhongshan Prince, Mancheng, Hebei, excavated in 1968, is also inscribed with *Yang Xin jia*; these were all the elder princess's private appliances. The gold-gilded Boshan incense burner from Ganquanshan, Yangzhou, Jiangsu, belonged to the Prince of Guangling of the Han Dynasty, from which we can see the extravagant life of the imperial household.

Lastly we should mention the bronzes of the ancient minorities. Earlier objects of the Kayue Culture have been indicated above; those articles of the northern people excavated from Inner Mongolia manifest the features of the prairie people. The dragon-head dagger from Xigoupan, Zhunge'er, Inner Mongolia, is of the Han Dynasty but has the lines of the Shang Dynasty. Similar Shang daggers of this sort from Haocheng, Hebei; Shilou, Shanxi; and Suide and Qingjian of Shaanxi indicate the tradition of the blood relationship and culture among the people.

The Han tombs excavated at Laoheshen, Yushu, Jilin, in 1981 may belong to the ancient Xianbei Nationality. The bronze-handled iron sword on exhibit is different from that of the Central Regions while the two mirrors, one with 4 nipples and 8 birds, the other with 7 nipples, are typical of the Han style—proof of the influence of the culture of the Central Regions.

Southern bronzes of the Bashu Culture have been mentioned above. The bronze drum and the sheep-horn knobbed bell of Luobowan, Guixian, Guangxi, have their special features, but the lamp of 9 branches is no different from those of the Central Regions. Also worth mentioning are the objects from Guizhou and Yunnan. The Han Dynasty tombs at Kele, Hezhang, Guizhou, had been repeatedly excavated; the gilded cauldron (*mao*) on display is the same as those from other regions except for its three small feet, which are unusual. The salamander-shaped buckle from Weining, a neighbouring county of Hezhang, is typical of local style.

Recently unearthed rare relics on this exhibition are rich and varied, but this is only a part of the new finds which have already pointed out the long stride our archaeologists have been making. I am sure we are going to have a still wider and finer display in the near future.

ers were able to handle the depth of landscape painting. This is also the earliest blue and green mineral-coloured landscape painting existing.

Qian Li Jiang Shan Tu (The Picture of a Thousand *Li* Scope Waters and Mountains) by Wang Ximeng of the Northern Song Dynasty is an outstanding landscape painting. The painter created the painting at the age of eighteen. The mineral-coloured picture shines with a lustre as beautiful as precious stone, giving a majestic view of the country. This further developed the art of traditional mineral blue-green landscape painting.

Xiao Xiang Tu (The Southern Landscape) by Dong Yuan of the Five Dynasties is an excellent ink and wash painting. In the near distance, men are ferrying and fishing in the river; farther are the grass and trees on the hilly land; in the mist of fog and clouds, the scenery of a moist water village is very well depicted. Following in his footsteps was monk Ju Ran; they are jointly mentioned in painting history as founders of the school which became the mainstream of landscape painting in the Ming and Qing dynasties.

Xiao Xiang Qi Guan Tu (The Wonderful Southern Scenery) by Mi Youren is a representative work of ink and wash painting showing the free-hand brushwork depicting the mist and clouds scenery of the south. Mi maintained that a painter should have his own individuality; in this picture we can see the freehand random dots touching up the mist, clouds, far forests and mountains at the joint of the two rivers, Xiang and Xiao, in Hunan Province. Though colourless, it has the effect of a blue-green landscape painting.

The Five Dynasties is an important epoch for the

development of the Chinese painting. *The Portrait of Rare Birds* by Huang Quan, depicts more than ten different birds, two tortoises and some insects of different forms, all lifelike. Huang Quan's meticulous bright-coloured flower and bird painting, his style and technique offered a great influence to the palatial painting of the Song Dynasty.

Using a contrary technique is the portrait *Autumn Willow and Double Crows* by Liang Kai of the Southern Song Dynasty; by just a few free brushstrokes the posture of trees and bird flight in the autumn season is vividly portrayed on the small picture.

The store of the Ming and Qing paintings in the museum is of ample quantity, comprising the works of the palatial painters Lin Liang and Lü Ji; the scholar painters Shen Zhou, Wen Zhengming and Tang Yin of the Ming Dynasty; Zhu Da (Ba Da Shan Ren), the Yangzhou School painters, down to Ren Bonian and Wu Changshuo, etc., of later years.

Aside from the royal holds, the museum has bought a lot of private collections and accepted donations; mounters, repairers and facsimile reproducers are also employed in the museum. A research department has been formed to judge the value of ancient paintings and other cultural objects, and determine their positions in the history of Chinese art.

An Introduction to Ancient Chinese Bronze Mirrors

Du Naisong

The pursuit of beauty is human nature; labouring, man not only created his living materials but also brought forth the art of beauty. Ancient Chinese bronze mirrors were invented and developed in the pursuit of beauty. Like other objects of art, they reflect the culture, art, ideology, economy and social state of a period of time.

Mirrors were used to apply facial make-up. Most of them are rounded or square shaped; the face is finely polished and the back has a node and design. The beautiful designs reflect the custom and culture of the time as well as the technique of the artisans. In museums throughout the nation, the collection of bronze mirrors is numerous. The most part of them are newly excavated in recent years; they added radiant splendour to ancient Chinese culture.

In ancient documents, bronze mirrors were much noted. In *Shi Ming* (*The Book of Terminology*); "A mirror is an object to reflect your image." In *Qi Ce of Zhan Guo Ce* (*Discourses on Politics of the Warring States*), in the piece entitled "Zuo Ji Made Parables to the Prince of Qi to Accept his Advice", "When dressing up, look at the mirror." In the long narrative poem of the Northern and Southern Dynasties, "Mulan Joins the Army", a girl disguised herself as a boy and joined the army for her old father; having fought the enemy for ten years, she returned home and restored her usual costume. A stanza reads, "Behind the window I knit my bun; Facing the mirror I insert yellow flowers on it." In ancient paintings and on tomb murals like Gu Kaizhi's "Nü Shi Zhen Tu" and the Song tomb mural unearthed at Baisha, Yuxian County, Henan Province, bronze mirrors are depicted as women dress their hair, waited on by lady attendants—these are real portrayals of the employment of mirrors.

Since olden times, beautiful stories about mirrors are not few. The Tang poet Meng Qi's poem tells that during the fall of the Chen Dynasty (557-589), Xu Deyan and his wife, Princess Lechang, broke a mirror into two halves, each carrying one piece as a token. After an enforced separation, the broken mirror was joined together as husband and wife were reunited.

The ancient people were superstitious. Archaeologists have found that mirrors are often placed on top of a grave or at the four corners of a coffin; the people believed so doing might get rid of the evil spirits. The ancient people served the dead as the living; that is why so many mirrors are placed in tombs above the head or by the side of the chest, which shows that they are for daily use. In a Song tomb, excavated few years ago, there is a mirror-holding figurine which shows that the dead woman expects to have a maid servant to attend her. In Changsha tombs, mirrors are in lacquer cases in the midst of wooden combs. In Xinjiang Han and Guangzhou Nanyue tombs, mirrors are in silk wrappers.

Mirrors were used when dressing up; later, the Chinese character "*jian*" (mirror) transferred its meaning to an object lesson, or as a kind of reflector. Tang Emperor Taizong (627-649), on Wei Zheng's death, spoke to his courtiers: "A bronze mirror can help you to be immaculately attired; taking history as a mirror, you can know the vicissitudes of the world; if you take man as a reflector, you can understand loss or gain. Usually I keep these three mirrors to correct my mistakes; now that Wei Zheng has died, I have lost one of my mirrors."

When was the bronze mirror first invented and employed in ancient times? *The Biography of Huangdi* remarked: "When the Emperor met the West Empress at the Mountains of Wangwu, twelve large mirrors were wrought for use month by month." But that was only an invented story. The word "mirror" has not been found among the inscriptions on bones and shells of the Shang Dynasty. However, the word *jian* has been found, indicating a kind of shallow vessel containing water for reflecting one's face. *Guang Ya* (an ancient dictionary) says, "*Jian* is a mirror."

Judging from recently excavated objects, the earliest mirror belongs to the Qijia Culture from about four thousand years ago, during the Xia Dynasty (2100-1600 B.C.); two very small and crude mirrors have been unearthed at Qijiaping, Guanghe County, Gansu Province, and separately at Duomatai, Guinan, Qinghai Province.

A few mirrors of the Shang Dynasty have also been found. In 1976, four mirrors were excavated from the No. 5 Tomb of the Yin Dynasty ruins, An'yang; their general characteristics are a small bow node and simple arc designs between which are straight lines; at the border there are nipples. In a certain degree they reflect a rustic style of mirror making in the embryonic stage.

Mirrors of the Western Zhou Dynasty to the Spring and Autumn Period have been unearthed not only in greater number but also from a wider scope of districts, mainly within the Yellow River valley. The general features of the more than ten mirrors excavated are a rather thin round shape, about 6-10 centimetres in diamenter with a small arc node, a flat back without decoration, and a slightly embossed rim. One thing worth mentioning is the double-node bird-and-animal designed mirror unearthed during 1956-57 at Shangcunling, Sanmenxia City, Henan Province. The design cast is a portrait of animals, with tigers, deer and birds which are realistic, vivid, and true to nature.

The use of mirrors was very common during the Warring States period, unlike earlier times. Its rise has much to do with the fall of the slave owning and the feudal systems of the Shang and Zhou dynasties, and the development of commodity production in the feudal society. The features of that period are the cutely made and mostly rounded shapes, but a small part of them are square shaped. An example is the hollow, carved, crouching-dragon designed, square mirror unearthed at Fengshushan, Changsha, Hunan Province. The coiled dragons are capering in many forms which are true to life and touching. Most of the flat-backed square mirrors from Fenshuiling, Changzhi, Shanxi Province, have very small fluted arc nodes. In the Palace Museum, there is a frognoded Warring

States mirror which is a rare object. Such mirrors often have a round or square base beneath the node. Most Warring States mirrors are not inscribed and have no design on the back. On some mirrors a single pattern covers the whole surface; others have double tiers of decorations, one of which is the main body while the other serves as a foil to it. The variety of designs is rich and colourful; according to preliminary examinations there are geometric designs, plumage patterns, coiled dragons, *shan* or inverted T, rhomboid patterns, four leaves, dragons and phoenixes, animals, hunting portraits, dragons and birds, etc.

The diameter of Warring States mirrors is generally small, however, the one found in Shangwangzhuang, Linzi, Shandong, in 1964, is as big as 29.8 centimetres, inlaid with malachites, cloud-patterned and multinoded. At the rim there are three ring nodes positioned like a tripod's feet; the curled lines of the clouds are gold gilt, inlaid with malachite and set with nine silver nipples (4 missing). Such a large diameter and fine make is quite rare among mirrors of this period. Another notable mirror was discovered in Jincun, Luoyang, Henan, before liberation; it is a silver- and gold-gilt hunting portrait—warriors on horseback, with swords in hands, struggling with leopards. The Qin mirror from Shuihudi (meaning The Spot Where the Tiger Sleeps), Yunmeng, Hubei, is a portrait of two warriors fighting leopards with shields and swords. The cloud-designed painted bronze mirror from the No. One Big Tomb of Changtaiguan, Xinyang, Henan, is a very beautiful bronze.

From the above we can see that mirrors of the Warring States period are not only greater in number and much better in quality, but also contain a sort of rhythmic beauty, particularly the Chu State's mirrors.

In the Western and Eastern Han era, owing to the development of iron, lacquer and pottery wares, many bronze wares had been superseded; but in some aspects fine bronzes still developed further, particularly in the making of mirrors, which became an important enterprise of the time.

In the beginning, the style still followed the convention of the Warring States; that is, the crouching dragons pattern was still in vogue. But a whirled-ground crouching dragon designed mirror has been found from the No. One Western Han Tomb of Mawangdui, Changsha, Hunan. The mirror was wrapped in a red silk cloth and placed in a round toilet case. The six *shan* (T) on plumage ground mirror was found in the tomb of the second king of the Nanyue Kingdom in the year 1984 at Xianggangshan, Guangzhou. The six-*shan* mirror is very rare, only one was ever recorded in *Yan Ku Cang Jing* in the past. The newest features of this epoch are the inscriptions of auspicious expressions on the back of the mirrors, comprised of three or four characters in a sentence, e.g.: "Think of each other long; ever forget each other and may you forever have high rank and wealth; Happiness never ending." There are also inscriptions such as "Long happiness never finishing," and "Great joy, nobility and wealth; A thousand autumns and ten thousand years; May you have wine and food," etc. Around the time of Han Emperor Wudi, the arc node became a semispherical node, with a persimmon-fruitbase as the base of the node; the border is broad and flat, and the mirror is thicker and heavier. During this time, mirrors of grass

Crouching-dragon-designed bronze mirror
of the Western Han Dynasty

leaves appeared, a design that must have been handed
down from the Warring States period; the astronomical
star and cloud patterned mirrors also arose. Recently
unearthed from a tomb dating from around the time of
Han Emperor Wudi at Zibo, Shandong, is a huge
rectangular mirror measuring 115 x 57.5 centimetres,
which must have been used for checking the full-length
view. What had been recorded in *Zhan Guo Ce* is
not false. The back has five nodes with persimmon-
fruitbase foundations, and is decorated with interwov-

en coiled dragons. The mirror from the Chang'an City ruins of the Han Dynasty at Xi'an has a coloured portrait on its back; on a vermilion background are chariots, horses and men out hunting. Such patterns on a mirror are quite unique.

After the Han Emperor Wudi era, there arose the sunlight and the Zhao Ming (bright) mirrors; their inscriptions are self-commending concerning the fine quality of the mirrors: "Seeing the light of the sun, the universe is very bright." "With the fine quality to shine, its brightness is like that of the sun or the moon." Some of the inscriptions coil the characters into two circles; the inner reads, "Seeing the light of the sun, never forget each other." The outer circle may read, "With the fine quality of its shining, its brightness is like that of the sun or moon. At once you are raised to loyalty, and to zeal which will never dissipate." At that time there also appeared mirrors of four nipples and four dragons, which were developed from the crouching dragon patterns. Worth mentioning is that some of these mirrors have a transparent effect; when light is cast on the surface, the design on the back is reflected on the wall. This is due to the casting curvature on the surface, which is invisible to the naked eye after being ground. The invention reflects the wisdom of the craftsmen of two thousand years ago.

The surface of mirrors of the Eastern Han, Wei, and Jin to the Northern and Southern dynasties was no longer a flat plate but slightly convex, which casts a better reflection. The persimmon-fruitbase foundation beneath the node is much more enlarged, somewhat like a bat. Popular fashions of this period were relief mythical animals and legendary figures, such as portraits of Wu Zixu, King of Yue State, and Fan Li, as well as the Empress of the West, Emperor of the East, the God of the Chariot, etc. Many are inscribed with auspices like, "May you forever have sons and grandsons," "You have the qualifications to be a high official," "May you attain the rank of three dukes," etc. Still more numerous are the long inscriptions, mingling auspicious words and workshop propaganda together: "Mirrors made by the Hous are generally perfect, engraved by skilled artisans to make them exquisite articles. Dragons on the left, tigers on the right to keep away evils, Seven sons and nine grandsons are in the middle. May the couple be forever in good health." A mirror from Yichang, Hubei, wrought at Guiji, the Wu Princedom, reads, "Work of the Baos. May be handed down for generations." Some are inscribed, "Copper from Xuzhou, Artisans from Luoyang." During this time, dated mirrors were also getting more numerous.

The Sui and Tang mirrors are very nice in quality, generally thick and heavy, fine and bright. Aside from round and square shapes, there were octagon, star thistle, square- and rounded-corner forms, and mirrors with a handle. The contents of the designs are immense, generally combining real life, mythology and the pursuit of a happy life in a portrait which offers people a fresh and pleased feeling. That was a long stride in the process of designing. The designs mainly are flowers and butterflies, grapes, birds and beasts, birds on a blossom, double phoenix, dragons in the clouds, fairies in the moon, stories of historical figures, polo playing, etc. Among personal stories there are mirrors of the three joys, formerly called mirrors of Rong Qiqi, which express a story from *Lie Zi* (one of

Bronze mirror of the Tang Dynasty with
the design of fairy-on-beasts-back

the pre-Qin schools of thought). Depicted on the mirror is Confucius conversing with an old man, Rong Qiqi, asking him, "What is joy?" To which the latter answered, "Longevity is a joy." In the Palace Museum there is a caltrop-flower mirror of polo, with four players on horseback hitting a small ball, which is quite vivid and interesting.

Among the Tang mirrors, some of the designs are also inlaid with gold, silver or mother-of-pearl on portraits of figures, landscapes or flowers, and birds, which are very colourful and of high artistic level. Some are inscribed, "One thousand autumns and ten thousand years." One excavated at Hefei, Anhui, bears the name of the maker—"By Li Cheng, copper workshop of the capital."

Song mirrors also developed to a certain extent; most are in caltrop, square or sunflower shapes; some of the round ones are very large in size. The designs are mainly entwined herbs and flowers or peony; there are also double fish, double phoenix and sailing designs. The mirror from the Liao Emperor's son-in-law,

Tang mirror of dragon design

Prince of Wei's tomb at Chifeng, has four butterflies. Mirrors of this time often have an advertisement of the workshop, e.g., "Mirror of peerless smelt copper by the Second Uncle Shi Nian of Huzhou," "Bronze mirror by the Gongs of Chengdu," and "Smelt copper mirror by the Maos of the Prefecture of Jiankang."

Most Yuan, Ming, and Qing mirrors imitate the Han and Tang, but double fish designs are more numerous. On the back of some Ming and Qing mirrors are lacquer-filled portraits and inscribed auspices, e.g.,

Ship-sailing-on-sea-waters-designed mirror
of the Song Dynasty

"May you have a noble son soon," "Age high as the mountains, blessings full as the sea," "May your age be as tall as the South Mountain," "Longevity, wealth and rank," "Come first in the imperial examination," etc. The one in the Palace Museum bears a stanza of seven-words verse, "Full as the moon, clear as water, Opening the mirror case, see your old friend."

During the rign of Qianlong (1736-95), the glass mirror became widely used and took the place of copper. From that time the production of bronze mirror gradually stopped.

Porcelain Vase with Reticulated Exterior and Independently Revolving Interior

Wang Liying

In the porcelain hall of the Palace Museum there is a unique hollowed-out vase which contains another smaller vase. When touched at its mouth, the inner vase revolves like paper-made animated pictures, showing the portraits of "A Foreigner Presents Treasures", "The Play of Sixteen Characters", etc.

Why does it revolve, and how was it placed into the outer vase? The axis is a chicken-heart knob and the groove under the inner bottom is of the same shape to match it. What a novelty device at the time! It was impossible to bake the whole thing in the kiln, because the axis and the groove would have gotten stuck. Actually, when making the embryo, the vase was crossed into three sections, which were put together after being painted and glazed.

Such porcelain wares were precious playthings in the palace of the Qing Dynasty, and rarely appeared beyond the palace. Most of them are large, such as vases of the *Yu Hu Chun* type (spring of the jade pot) or cylindrical shape. Generally, elephant ears, dragons, or phoenix designs are added at the neck to make the

Porcelain vase with reticulated exterior
and independently revolving interior

vase look more solemn. Four windows of various shapes are opened at the belly of the outer vase. Some of the outer vases are hollowed-out with meticulous designs of bats-in-clouds or dragons-in-clouds; with colours of sky-blue, dark blue, bright yellow, winter green or turquoise as the base, added to light blue, pink or purplish-carmine, off-setting each other very beautifully. Upon this foundation are painted butterflies, linked-lotus, crouching-dragons, or twined-herbs-and-flowers of powdered or golden glaze. Relative characters of Heavenly Stems and Earthly Branches are written amidst the patterns. Some of the glaze-bases are finely veined with phoenix-tail streaks or adorned with blue floral designs. Most inner vases are cylindrical, painted with portraits of children at play, foreigners presenting treasures, flowers of the four seasons, twined flowers, etc. Some are attached to ancient objects or decorated with a boat sailing on waves of the sea.

All revolving vases have inscriptions on the bottom, of blue, gold or red colour, "Made in the Qianlong years of the Great Qing" or "Made in the Qianlong years". Such vases were not made in a day. Ever since the Ming Dynasty artisans of the Longquan Kiln had made this article of celadon, and in the early days of the Qing, the art further developed. Nevertheless, the revolving device, solved by the artisans of the Jingdezhen Kiln, was a new break-through.

According to records, "On the 12th day of the 5th moon of the Qianlong 18th year, the emperor decreed the Jiangxi Kiln to make a revolving vase of dragonboats-racing and tumblers'-play patterns. The said vase was handed in on the 4th day of the 19 year." It took at least half a year to finish the work. However, in the history of porcelain making, such ware was only a flash in the pan. Following the decline of porcelain making, production stopped after the years of Qianlong. Since the birth of Chinese Republic in 1911, endeavours have been made to produce this kind of vase, but the efforts have never succeeded.

Gossip on Ancient Fans

Wang Laiyin

Fans are used for making a current of air to cool oneself in summer. In ancient times, rounded-silk and feather fans, which cannot be folded, were used in China. Reliable records noted that fans had been used in the Western Han Dynasty, but in fact they were in use much earlier than that. Fans are of various shapes —round, elongated round, oblate, rounded square, plum-flower, carbapple-flower, sunflower, etc. The coverings are made from thin silk, silk-gauze, thin damask, etc. From the Sui and Tang dynasties up to today, paper has also been used.

Fans are articles of handicraft art; calligraphers and painters like to write or paint on the covering of fans. Wang Xizhi, Su Shi, and other noted scholars all wrote or painted on fans; literary works also described the beauty of fans.

The handles of fans are varied arts of jade, ivory, wood, bone, bamboo, red sandalwood and lacquer sculptures. In 1975, two rounded fans were excavated from Zhou Yu's tomb of the Southern Song Dynasty at Jintan County, Jiangsu Province; both are elongated with thin wooden shafts, backed with bamboo strips. Both are covered by paper which has turned brown with age. One of the handles is a hollowed-out lacquer sculpture, which is a precious artifact in the technological history of lacquer engraving.

The folding fan is not generally regarded as a Chinese creation, but one imported from Japan during the Song Dynasty. But others regard it as of Chinese origin, which assumption needs further proof. Japanese folding fans were sold in the noted market of the Daxiangguo Monastery at Kaifeng, the metropolis of the Northern Song Dynasty; after that time, Chinese folding fans became well developed and popularly used, particularly among the literati and officialdom. The making had also been improved; the number of ribs increased from 5, 7, 8, to 10 or more. The art of carving also was elevated, with patterns more decorative than before. Ivory and sandalwood fans have been designed typically of Chinese style.

The earliest and biggest folding fan of China is now in the Palace Museum. It has fifteen ribs, the two outer ones being much broader, 82 centimetres long; the covering is 59.5 centimetres high and 152 centimetres long. The top of the outer ribs is a little narrower than the bottom; the ribs have square heads and rounded bottoms, quite unlike today's folding fans. All of the exposed parts of the ribs are veneered with the skin mottled bamboo (*Xiangfeizhu*). On the paper covering are painted coloured figures; a black-gauze-capped master admires flowers under the willow shade, while a servant holding a vase in both hands comes to his master; on the other side of the fan master and servant read under a pine tree. It is further inscribed with "Painted by the Emperor in a spring day of the second year of Xuande, in the Hall of Military Brilliancy (Wuyingdian)." Two chops of Emperor Qianlong are put on the painting. Zhu Zhanji (1398-1435), who reigned for the last ten years of his life, was skillful in painting landscapes, figures, flowers and insects; under his patronage the Ming palatial painting prospered. This fan is a good reference in the research of folding fans and the Emperor's painting.

This big fan was not from the hands of ordinary artisans. It is the only one preserved in the palace and was found on October 13, 1949, in the south store room of Yangxindian Hall; although much damaged when found, it was later repaired. Such a big fan would not have been waved by the emperor himself, of course, but by his attendants; or it could have been made merely for his admiration, as a knick-knack.

Among other ancient folding fans there is an album of flattened coverings painted and written by Shen Zhou (1427-1509) and Wu Kuan (1435-1504) respectively; both were most noted artists of the Ming Dynasty. Recently excavated from Jiangyin County, Jiangsu Province, is a paper-cut bamboo folding fan of the Ming Dynasty. It has a plain covering, but when the fan is held up to sunlight, a paper cut portrait of "Plum and Magpie Announcing the Arrival of Spring" sandwiched between the surfaces is visible. Together with the fan there was a grain receipt book, on the front page of which characters were written "the twelfth year of Zhengde". From this we know the said fan is from no later than 1515. As well as these, in the Yangzhou Museum there is a fan written in the thirteenth year of Jiajing (1534), by Wu Cheng'en, author of *Xi You Ji* (*Pilgrimage to the West*). This rare relic was donated to the museum by Mr. Li Shengfu. In recent years, three folding fans were unearthed from the joint tomb of Wang Xijue at Huqiu, Suzhou. Wang Xijue died in 1610, his wife, Zhu, in 1598, and they were jointly buried in 1613. The fan for a man's use is 16-ribbed, 9 *cun* long, rounded waterstone-ground bamboo outer-ribbed, with calligraphy and painting on the paper covering; it is a pity the covering is ruined. The two for a lady's use are 22-ribbed, 9 *cun* long, rounded black-lacquer gold-dotted bamboo outer-ribbed, and have black coverings with golden dots and big-and-small lozenge designs on them. These two fans have been well preserved, and are as fresh as new. All of these fans are later than the big fan of the Ming Dynasty now in the Palace Museum.

In China, the history of fan use goes back into the remote past; fans of many varieties are skillfully made and decorated with calligraphy and painting, reflecting the glamour of ancient Chinese culture.

The Huge Bronze Buddha of Zhengding

Li Jinbo

In the city of Zhengding County, Hebei Province, stands the Longxing Temple, which was built in the 6th year of Kaihuang of the Sui Dynasty (586), 1,400 years ago.

In North China, Longxing Temple may not be very famous, but the big Buddha inside is known to everyone. It is no wonder that people regard the Changzhou Lion, Dingzhou Pagoda, and Dingzhou Big Buddha together with the Zhaozhou large stone bridge as four treasures of North China. The big Buddha is an overall bronze cast, 22 metres tall, erected in the main hall of Dabeige (the Hall of Great Mercy). It is second in size only to the Buddha in Tibet, which is just 40 centimetres taller. It has 42 arms, holding magic weapons of the sun, the moon, the clean vase, sword, wand, mirror, white whisk, Buddha warrior's club, etc. Hence the name of "A Thousand-Handed and -Eyed Bodhisattva". The Buddha's ear, reached via a steep, stone staircase from the hall, is bigger than a man. In spite of the gigantic size, the statue was made in accurate proportions of graceful contour; its facial expression is solemn and calm. All of these shows the wit and the creative spirit of the ancient artists.

As inscribed in the monument, the hall of the temple was burnt to ashes and the upper part of the Buddha was melted into scraps during 944 when the nationality Qidan was attacking China proper. In 955, the second year of Xiande of the Later Zhou Dynasty, Emperor Zhou Shizhong ordered the Buddha smelted to mint coins. At that time, the bronze Buddha became a clay Buddha.

In 969, when the first emperor of the Song Dynasty visited the temple, Abbot Kechuo complained to him

The Huge Bronze Buddha of Zhengding

about the misfortune of the bronze Buddha and invented a story, saying that upon its demolition a mysterious oracle of eight big characters had appeared on the Buddha's lotus throne: "Perish when meeting with Xian (*Xiande* year), but revive when the Song (Dynasty) is encountered." Zhao Kuangyin (the emperor) was pleased to order the rebuilding of the temple and the Buddha. The construction started on the lunar 20th date of the 7th moon in the year 971; three thousand soldiers and civilians toiled on it.

The foundation was laid by digging deep to the groundwater level and then ramming layers of gravel and earth one after another to two metres below ground level. The pit is 13 metres square and 2 metres deep; into it 7 wrought iron piles were driven; then the whole pit was cast with pig iron.

Design drawings of the Buddha had been submitted to the emperor three times for his approval. The Buddha was cast in seven sections up from the bottom. The first section is the lotus throne; the feet and knees are the second section, then to the navel, chest, arm-pit, shoulders, and the top of the head. It was said when reaching the shoulder part, the molten copper would solidify as it was raised, and workers did not know what to do. They asked for advice from an old man who had been watching their work. The old man answered, "I have been buried to the neck, what can I do for you!" Inspired by the words, workers buried the body to the neck with soil and thus the Buddha was made. The story might not be true, but the hardship of handicraft production of a thousand years ago is within our comprehension.

The method of making the 42 arms was to cast

tubes first, then insert wooden hands into them and cover the entire arm with gold foil. It is a pity that in the early decades of the Qing Dynasty, all of the arms, except the two before the chest, were cut down; in 1944, wooden arms were refitted.

Through a thousand years of building the huge Buddha, labouring people's misfortune had not been relieved. Nevertheless, they left us this treasure of art, a symbol of their skill, glittering for a thousand years.

The Noninscribed Monument of Qianling

Liu Zhaoyi

Not far from the city of Xi'an, one can see numerous burial mounds of the ancient emperors. At the foot of Lishan Mountain is the tomb of Qin Shi Huang the First Emperor of the Qin Dynasty (221-207 B.C.); to the northeast of Xingping County is the tomb of Han Emperor Wudi (Maoling). All of these were heaped up with earth, making a grand sight to look at from afar. However, among all the mounds, the most attractive to travellers is Qianling, one of the 18 Tang Tomb Mounds.

The 18 Tang Tomb Mounds were built on the plateau north of the Wei River in the near counties of Xi'an. For the sake of security, the second emperor didn't build his tomb by heaping earth but had himself buried in the bosom of a mountain. However, all of the tombs, except Qianling, were robbed during the Five Dynasties period.

Qianling is on Liangshan Mountain in the north of Qianxian City, 80 miles from Xi'an. It is a joint tomb of Tang Emperor Gaozong and his wife Wu Zetian. Wu Zetian was a concubine of Tang Emperor Taizong, after whose death she became a nun. In 655, she was made queen by the old emperor's son Tang Emperor Gaozong, the third emperor of the Tang Dynasty. He was sick at the end of his life, and she became the actual ruler. She even changed the title of the dynasty and made herself the only woman emperor of China.

Qianling is comprised of three peaks; the southern two peaks form a natural gate and the northern peak is the tomb proper. The tomb covers more than three hundred thousand *mu* of land, surrounded by double-fold city walls, and had 378 rooms. To the southeast of Qianling are 17 accompanying burials of princes and ministers. In the courtyard there still stand groups of huge stone figurines. From south to north there are a pair of octagonal columns, a pair of winged horses and a pair of rosefinches, five pairs of stone horses, ten pairs of capped and robed stone generals with swords in hands, and 61 envoys and rulers of minorities and friendly countries who had attended the funeral of Tang Emperor Gaozong. All of the sculptures are true and life like.

There are two monuments, both 6.3 metres tall. The western one was for the emperor, and was constructed of seven sections of stone. The inscription was composed by his wife and written by his son, eulogizing his ruling career. On the east is the Non-inscribed Monument, built from a whole piece of stone. Wu Zetian erected it for herself, but not a word was inscribed on it. By so doing, she indicated that her greatness couldn't be expressed by words. Others say that she was modest, leaving everything to be commented upon by the forthcoming generations. This theory modernizes Wu Zetian. Nevertheless, the wordless monument has since been inscribed by literary travellers of the Song and Kin dynasties; they merely noted their travels but never had a word on the woman emperor. So we say she was a clever woman, because otherwise there would be many disputes about her. Therefore, the lack of an inscription has been better for her historic reputation than an inscription would have been.

Luckily, the tomb of Wu Zetian hadn't been robbed up to today. What treasure they have in the underground palace is still unknown. But several of the 17 accompanying tombs have been excavated—the tomb of Princess Yongtai, Li Xianhui; the tomb of Crown Prince Zhanghuai, Li Xian; the tomb of Prince Yide, Li Congyun; the tomb of Grand Secretary Xue Yuanchao and the tomb of General Li Jinxing. A large quantity of frescoes, tricoloured porcelains, stone engravings and other important relics have been unearthed. Relics from the Princess's tomb are of the greatest number. She is a granddaughter of Wu Zetian, who died at 17, the monument says, of difficult labour. But folk history says she was killed because she criticized her granny. From her tomb, a large amount of tri-coloured pottery, colour-painted figurines, figures on horseback, tri-coloured horses, tapestry and frescoes have been put on display. The fresco "Maids of Honour" has 16 beautiful maids of different manners, brilliantly coloured with skill. From this tomb alone we have found such a lot of beautiful things. The whole world will be dumbfounded when the underground treasure of Qianling is open to the public view.

The World-Renowned Bridge of Lugouqiao

Luo Zhewen

From the Ferry of Lugou to the Construction of the Bridge

The district of Lugouqiao was the vital communication line from the North China plain to the northeastern regions of China. For countless generations our ancestors lived and laboured here. Not far to the southwest of Lugouqiao is Zhoukoudian where Peking Man lived half a million years ago. Not far to the south is Liulihe where a large number of burials, chariot pits and bronzes of the Western Zhou Dynasty have been excavated. According to records, the present district of Beijing, which is to the northeast of Lugouqiao, was the political centre of the Yan State in the Warring States Period. Since then, the area, added with the neighbouring Jixian County district, has been important for many successive dynasties. But the traffic on the road along the eastern foot of Taihang Mountain leading to spots of north China is interrupted by the turbulent waves of the great Lugou River transversing from the west to the southeast. Over the years, the Lugou Ferry was established at this mountain pass where the flow of the Yongding River, down from Guanting through ridges and gorges, has become more silent and easy to cross.

The Yongding (Ever Stable) River has a phase of extraordinary history related to the Bridge of Lugouqiao. Lugou (the ditch of Mount Lushi), also known as Sangganhe (the river of Sanggan), is a branch of the ancient Leishui (the stream of Lei). It originates from Mount Leishan of Mayi County, Shanxi Province. When northwest of Beijing, it passes along the west side of Mount Lushi, hence the name of Lugou. Because the stream is turbid and overflows at times, and the river course often changes, this river is also called Wudinghe (the uncertain river). In 1698, the stream was thoroughly dredged and dykes reinforced to prevent inundations; therefore the new name, Yongding River, was given to it. But at the end of the Qing Dynasty, owing to negligence in dredging, the river collapsed again. Since the birth of New China in 1949, a reservoir has been built at Guanting and the embankment strengthened; only now has the river become ever stable.

"Notes on the Travel of the Envoy to the Kin State in the Year of Yi Si, Xuanhe" of Xu Kangzong of the Song Dynasty recorded that in the year 1125 when he crossed the Lugou Ferry, the stream was quite turbulent. People could only cross the waters on a temporary bridge or a floating bridge depending on the height of the water level. At the time, it was very busy at the ferry; inns and shops had been built on the banks to provide lodgings for passengers.

Following the development of the social economy, when Beijing was made capital by the Kin Dynasty in 1153, the ferry could no longer meet the demand for the traffic between the north plains and south China —referring mainly to land transportation. In 1189, a decree was issued to have a permanent stone bridge built on the spot. In three years the work was completed and the bridge was called Guangliqiao (the vastly benefited bridge). But the general public still call Lugouqiao, referring to the bridge and the place as well. Described by Marco Polo, the bridge has been known to the world for six hundred years. On July 7, 1937, the resistance to Japanese invasion also started here. Since 1949, this bridge has been preserved as a key cultural relic.

The Scenery of "the Morning Moon over the Lugou River" and Marco Polo's Description of the Bridge

The bridge has 11 arches and a total length of 266.5 metres. It is the oldest stone bridge in north China and a precise, fine work from the very beginning of its construction. There are numerous fine stone sculptures —columns, parapets, lions, etc.

For seven hundred years, "the Morning Moon over the Lugou River" has been one of the eight scenic spots of Yanjing (Beijing). Emperor Qianlong of the Qing Dynasty wrote a monument on the end of the bridge. "It was not the colour of the morning moon that made the scenery but the joy of arrival at the destination." The location of the bridge was a traffic centre about fifteen kilometres away from the capital. Starting at dawn, it was just a day's journey to enter the city. Merchants, despatch-riders and candidates for the imperial examination, having stayed overnight, commenced their journey on the bridge under the moonlight, thus making the scenery famous.

Marco Polo, an official in the Yuan court for more than twenty years, described the bridge as follows:

"Upon leaving the capital and travelling ten miles, you come to a river named Pulisangan (the Sanggan River), which discharges itself into the ocean, and is navigated by many vessels entering from thence, with considerable quantities of merchandise. Over the river there is a very handsome bridge of stone, perhaps unequalled by another in the world. Its length is three hundred paces, and its width eight paces; so that ten men can, without inconvenience, ride abreast.... On each side, and from one extremity to the other, there is a handsome parapet, formed of marble slabs and pillars arranged in a masterly style. At the commencement of the ascent the bridge is something wider than at the summit, but from the part where the ascent terminates, the sides run in straight lines and parallel to each other. Upon the upper level there is a massive and lofty column, resting upon a tortoise of marble, and having near its base a large figure of a lion, with a lion also on the top. Towards the slope of the bridge there is another handsome column of pillar, with its lion, at the distance of a pace and a half from the former; and all the spaces between one pillar and another, throughout the whole length of the bridge, are filled up with slabs of marble, curiously sculptured, and mortised into the next adjoining pillars,

101

which are, in like manner, a pace and a half asunder, and equally surmounted with lions, forming altogether a beautiful spectacle. These parapets serve to prevent accidents that might otherwise happen to passengers. What has been said applies to the descent as well as to the ascent of the bridge."

Apart from tourists and poets, painters also had portrayed the scenery of Lugouqiao Bridge. In the Chinese History Museum there is a Yuan painting, *Log-rafting on the Lugou River*, which takes the bridge as the main theme; log rafting is busy under the bridge, despatch-riders are running on the bridge, rows of inns and wine shops are at the two ends of the bridge, the hustling scene of six hundred years ago is still before your eyes. Columns, parapets, lions and elephants are exactly as they are today.

Why "Lugouqiao's Lions—Innumerable"

In the vicinity of Beijing there is a two-part allegorical saying, "Lugouqiao's lions—innumerable", which has been used for four or five hundred years. In *Chang An Ke Hua* (*The Capital Visitor's Talk*), "the lions on the parapets have a hundred postures, there is always one hidden away when you count them." *Di Jing Jing Wu Lue* (*Scenery of the Imperial Capital*) also says, "they are innumerable when you count them." Because there are so many lions of different forms, sizes and positions, when passers by count them at random in a short while, of course, one or two of them might be neglected.

In fact, they can be numbered exactly. In 1962,

they were counted in four categories, with the total number 485: big lions on the parapet pillars, 281; small lions on big lion's body, 198; 2 giant lions leaning against the parapets at the east end of the bridge; 4 lions on the top of columns.

Those stone lions are very lively sculptures; each of the 281 on the pillars has its own form. Some are chin up looking at the sky; some are gazing at the bridge; some turn their bodies seeming to have a talk with their neighbours; some are petting their young; the one on the southern parapet of the east end has one ear erect, listening to the water flow and talking with passengers. Female lions play with their cubs while males are playing with balls made of strips of silk.

Small lions are numerous, as big as several centimetres to more than ten centimetres long. There are two or three in a group, crawling on the body of a big lion. Some are on the head or on the back, or fighting in the lap. Others are running fast on the back, only half a head or a mouth appears; some are playing with bells or balls on the big lion's body. It would be very easy to neglect them when counting. That is why the saying goes, "Lugouqiao's lions—innumerable."

Aside from lions, there are also two stone monuments, both written by Emperor Qianlong. The one on the east end bears four big letters "Lu Gou Xiao Yue" (the Morning Moon over the Lugou River). The west one is a poem on the inspection of the Yongding River. The monument on the east was erected in the eighth year of Kangxi; the other on the west dates to the rebuilding of the bridge. All are important documents on the history and repair of the bridge.

The cross section of the bridge is 7.5 metres; including parapets and slab spans, the total length is 9.3 metres. The bridge is slightly raised in the middle, 93.5 centimetres higher than the level at the foot of parapets, about a slope of eight per thousand. The entrances are trumpet shaped; the widest start is 32 metres while the side diagonal is 28.2 metres. The slope is somewhat big, 2.13 metres at the summit, having a slope of 3.5 per hundred.

Owing to the frequent passing of carts and horses, the wear on the bridge was great, necessitating constant repair. But through inspection we find that a large part of the parapets, lions, columns and spanning slabs are still well preserved originals of six or seven hundred years ago.

Mural Paintings in Fahai Monastery, Beijing

Pan Jiezi

Shijingshan, in the west of Beijing, is a hustling city of steel, but near it is Cuiwei Hill, covered by forests of cypresses and pines. In the recess of the hill is Fahai Monastery, which is known to the world for its murals.

Fahai Monastery was built in 1437, in the village of Moshikou on the slope of the hill. It was supervised by Ming Emperor Zhu Qizhen's eunuch and close advisor, Li Tong, who managed both to please his master and collect money for himself out of the project. By dint of the royal force, he summoned all of the famous artisans and great craftsmen, spent immense funds, and took five years to complete the work. The imperial monastery was very majestic, comprising four grand halls, bell and drum tower, monks' dormitory, and scripture reciting rooms as well as the splendid frescoes which had exhausted all the energies of the great artisans.

Regretfully, much has changed in five hundred years; only the main hall and another hall are left between two giant white pines. The halls are covered with yellow glazed tiles, which still look as magnificent as they were in old days. The statues no longer exist but the frescoes are still well preserved. In the dark main hall, the stories of the painting, the bright colouring of the mineral pigments, the gold gilt and the masterly atmosphere have attracted numerous believers and tourists, both in the past and today.

Behind the shrine, painted on the middle of the back wall is the portrait of solemn-faced Goddess Guanyin, clad in gauze. She is sitting on a rock with water and clouds as the background, adorned by bamboo and peony, and attended by the boy Shancai and the warrior Weituo. On the right is Wenshu Buddha attended by disciples, a lion and a tamer. On the left is Puxian Buddha, also accompanied by disciples, a white elephant and a tamer. The Buddhas are great in size and solemn of mien, while the attendants are much smaller and very respectful, expressing the concept of class in Buddhism. By the sides of the back door are portraits of pilgrimage; on the left there are 16 persons led by a fairy with flowers in her hand; on the right are 19 sages led by a fairy with a coral vase in her hand. They are pacing forward in the midst of coloured clouds. The two groups of figures are arranged in orderly rows; each has a different expression: solemn, elegant, grave, generous, or interested in each other. The painting is vivid and touching, exhibiting to its viewers the magnificent phenomena in heaven. On the east and west flank walls are different Buddhas and flying Apsaras. These frescoes originally were the background paintings behind the 18 arhat statues. Some of their colours are still as fresh as new, but their artistic level is slightly lower than that on the back walls.

I have seen quite a lot of frescoes of the Ming Dynasty, but those in Fahai Monastery are the best, both in skill and the state of preservation. Ever since the reign of Yongle, famous painters had been gathered to the court, where they had previous artists' examples to follow, hence the nice result. I have visited Fahai Monastery many times and from each visit I have had a new gain. It reminds me of a story out of painting history: after viewing Zhang Senyou's painting on the first day, Yan Liben said, "He merely has an undeserved reputation." The next day Yan went again and said, "Anyhow, he is a capable hand among the contemporaries." But on the third day he said, "He deserves the reputation!" There Yan stayed for ten days; he wouldn't leave. With the Fahai Monastery paintings I have the same feeling.

The wall surface of the main hall is very coarse while the drawing lines are quite graceful. Some of the refined parts were carried out by freehand brushwork rather than by stiff drawings. Designs of clothes are complicated but not rigid, shadings are dyed in gradation, everything is perfect. Particularly striking is the draped gauze worn by Goddess Guanyin, drawn with white lines as thin as spider's silk, which is superlative craftsmanship indeed. The modelling of figures is accurate; the naked parts such as the face, breast, belly, arms, legs, hands and feet especially are contoured with variable lines, distinguishing the physiological features between men and women, sometimes a little exaggerated, in order to increase their beauty. Clouds, waters, trees, rocks, flowers and herbs are used as the background; they are also outlined with different kinds of lines to bring out their individual feel. The whole work was constructed with sharp contrast of colours, making the general appearance of the painting harmonious and exceedingly brilliant. Profound merits of art are not detectable without meticulous observation. I dare say the existing paintings in Fahai Monastery are peerless among the Ming murals.

1 The Boy Attendant Shancai.

2 The Girl Attendant with a Basket of Flowers.

3 Goddess with a Thousand Hands.

4 Goddess Guanyin with a Wheel-at-will.

Advances of Chinese Palaeoanthropology

Jia Lanpo

The Chinese nation has a long history. Long, long ago, ancestors of the Chinese nation were interested in seeking for the origin and development of mankind; mythology and folk-lore regarding human origin are the best witness. Assumptions had been made by naive materialists, but under small productivity a modern science could not be established. Following the importation of Western learnings, Chinese palaeoanthropology generated. With the excavation of Zhoukoudian as a foundation, progress has been made, particularly in recent decades.

First Dawning

Following the advance of modern capitalism in China during the period between the 19th and 20th century, Chinese forerunners tolled the bell of alarm and introduced Western learnings to their countrymen. Yan Fu (1853-1921) translated *Evolution* and Lu Xun (1881-1936) wrote an essay on *The History of Mankind*, explaining Hegel's and Darwin's theories, but under the feudal reign such principles could hardly be accepted.

Before this century, no remnants of the Stone Age had been published. In 1915, a Japanese professor, Tolii Lyuzou, wrote an article entitled "Early Races of Nanman (South Manchuria)", in which he pointed out that all the stone implements excavated at the spot were made or used even later than the Qin and Han dynasties: they were used by earlier Mongolians.

In 1921, in spite of the discoveries at Yunnan, Sichuan, Mongolia, etc., Max Loehr in his *Chinese Ancient Jade* denied the existence of the Chinese nation in the Stone Age, and further said that if there had been any Stone Age inhabitants of China, they belonged to nations other than the Chinese. Even in 1927, geologist Zhang Hongzhao in his *Shi Ya* (*On Stone Implements*) only admitted that they might belong to the New Stone Age.

It was the geologists who fought the first battle. Swedish scholar Johan Gunnar Andersson, under the supervision of the Institute of Geological Investigation, Ministry of Agriculture and Commerce, in 1919 started the investigation of the Chinese cultures in remote antiquity. The next year, in his first report, he filled out the sites where stone tools had been unearthed; among them, the discovery of the Yangshao Culture was the most attractive.

Specimen collector Liu Changshan took back hundreds of specimens from Yangshao Village, Mianchi County, Henan Province. He and Johan Gunnar Andersson went there in April 1921 to excavate ground tools, coloured and grey pottery fragments and numerous other objects. They worked there for more than a month. In the autumn of the same year, Chinese geol-

110

ogist Yuan Fuli, Canadian anatomist Davidson Black and Austrain palaeontologist Otto Zdansky made wider investigations and dated the Yangshao Culture to six thousand years ago. Another site at Shaguotun, Jinxi County, Liaoning Province, also belonged to the culture of the New Stone Age. In the cavern, Bai Wanyu found tools and human remains.

In 1920 at Qingyang County, Gansu Province, at the depth of 7.3 metres in yellow soil, a French Catholic priest, Emile Licent, discovered a human-struck quartzite tool. In the same year, at Zhaojiacha (35 kilometres north to the city), 24 metres below ground level in the gravel stratum, he further found two small slabs artificially peeled off from a quartzite tool. All of these belonged to the Old Stone Age.

Since then, excavations have occurred in large number. In 1922-23, at Shuidonggou, Lingwu County, Ningxia Province, and at Salawusu, Wushenqi, Inner Mongolia, French palaeontologist Teilhard de Chardin and Licent discovered large batches of fossils of vertebrates and stone implements. When examining the fossils from Salawusu, they found a human tooth, an outer upper left incisor of a 7- or 8-year-old child. This was the first find of intellectual mankind's fossil in China; Chinese scholars call it the Hetao Man, corresponding to the advancing Le Moustier Culture and the initial Aurignac Culture of Europe.

In the late 50's, Wang Yuping went several times to Salawusu and Shuidonggou to make investigations. In 1960, Hu Shouyong, Ji Hongxiang and Gai Pei went to Shuidonggou and obtained 2,000 tools which were determined by Jia Lanpo, Gai Pei and Li Yanxian to belong to the later period of the Old Stone Age. In

1963, the Zhiyu Site, Suxian, Shanxi, of 28,000 years ago was found and was determined to be from about the same time or a little later than Salawusu, because the accompanying mammals were much the same. In 1974, Jia Lanpo and Wei Qi also visited Shuidonggou; Jia Lanpo's impression was that Shuidonggou and Salawusu were not of the same period, that the former was still a little newer.

It was quite unexpectedly that such a small tooth aroused world attention; scholars, at home and abroad, all intend to seek for the treasure buried in the vast land of China.

Foundation Laid

Zhoukoudian is a mere small mountain village, in contrast to the magnificent city of Beijing or the scenery of Guilin. It is known to the world because the upright-standing Peking Man once dwelt there. People come here to experience the hardships of their ancestors' lives, and take up the torch of the Peking Man to run their own section with stronger energy.

In 1914, Andersson came to Peking as a mining adviser and found fossils of small mammals at Jigushan, Zhoukoudian. In 1919 the May 4th Movement of the call of science and democracy took place. In 1921 and 1923, Andersson together with Zdansky and Water Granger on the First Spot of Zhoukoudian found quartzite implement fragments under his feet; the fragments were not produced at the spot. He presumed that they must have been conveyed there by mankind, which theory was proven eight years later when Professor Pei Wenzhong discovered the first skull of Peking Man.

From 1927 excavations continued for 18 years. Bone fragments found could represent more than 40 men; about a hundred thousand implements or semi-implements, numerous bone and horn tools and fossils of a hundred kinds of vertebrates had been found; besides, there was evidence of the employment of fire. This is an immense treasure house beyond any evaluation. But here we have two points to stress:

In the first place, so many finds confirmed the validity of Java Man. Before that, there were not enough human fossils to justify the theory of evolution, nor to deny the traditional theological belief that men are created by God.

In the human evolution tree, Hegel invented a term, *Pithecanthropus adalus*, meaning "mute ape man" and inserted it between ape and man. When the Java Man was found Eugene Dubois gave it this name, but people disputed was it the skull of an ape or a man? Eugene Dubois was indignant and locked the specimen into a safe for 28 years. On December 1929, the finds at Zhoukoudian justified the belief in the dawing of mankind, and made people believe the existence of the upright standing men; they were the offspring of the Southern Ape and the ancestors of the Intellectual Man.

Secondly, the excavation brought forth good results and qualified personnel, laying the foundation for the establishment of the Chinese palaeoanthropology. Zhoukoudian was known to the world not only because of the finds of Peking Man and his culture but also the 24 nearby fossil spots within the range of 4 square kilometres, representing men of ten million to ten thousand years ago. Aside from the Peking Man spot, there were also Spots 13, 15 and 4 as well as the site where the Upper Cave Man of 18,000 years ago was found. Those finds have much to do with the research of the 4th Geological Era; for the time being, excavations still continue.

Two generations of specialists have come to prominence due to the Zhoukoudian excavations: aside from the above mentioned Pei Wenzhong, there are Li Jie, palaeo-vertebratist Yang Zhongjiang, geologists Bian Meinian, Jia Lanpo, and Li Yueyan; palaeo-ichthyologist Liu Xianting and other experts Li Yanxian, Zhao Zikui, Yuan Zhenxin, Lin Shenglong, Huang Weiwen, etc. Those who have researched the fossils of Peking Man and palaeovertebrates, and the exact geological period of Zhoukoudian, are much greater in number and they have published an immense number of theses. Because from the very beginning the excavation work was conducted according to strict scientific method, many skilful hands in fossil searching, excavating and repairing have been trained up. At the time, the excavation was led by the Geological Investigation Institute which was the predecessor of the present Institute of Palaeo-vertebrates and Palaeoanthropology, which has 200 on staff now. The excavation of Zhoukoudian has also given an impetus to the development of the research on the Chinese 4th Period geology. Some say that Yang Zhongjian and Pei Wenzhong, etc., are the founders of Chinese palaeoanthropology and palaeovertebrates. That is a just evaluation, because they did a lot of work in that respect. At present, excavations are taking place throughout

China; it was the Peking Man excavation that paved the way for the exploration.

Looking Forward to the Future

Since 1927, Chinese palaeoanthropology has come quite a great length, but up to now has still lagged behind the world standard. In recent decades, many new sites have been discovered, but research has been made largely by the qualitative description method. New techniques have been employed, but the progress is quite slow. Henceforth, poly-sciences infiltration method must be adopted in the study of palaeoanthropology. When human fossil remains are found, the environment of their stratum ought to be observed. We are now analysing spore pollen in order to know the features of the vegetation while the ancient men were living, so that we could make assumptions about the climate of a definite spot.

Testing the size of a deposit and the percentage of stable and unstable minerals can help us infer the climatic states in the deposit. Under different circumstances of deposit, in reaction to mechanical abrasion and chemical corrosion or depositing action, traces have been left on the minor structure of the sand surface. Through a scanning microscope we can identify the different circumstances of deposit—glacier, rivers, lakes, wind erosion, seashores, etc. Combining the study of the geological phenomena and the ancient ecology of plants and animals, we can accurately determine the natural environment of previously living things and mankind. Just now, we are starting the work in this respect.

In the research of stone implements, the microscopic method ought to be employed. Some are studying the function of stone implements; if successful, they will have made a greater stride than judging its use merely from the shape of the tool. Observation of the edge of a tool with a microscope was first conducted by Smirnov of Soviet Russia. His "Prehistorical Techniques", published in 1964, reported how he and his colleagues were trying to realize the function of a tool according to the traces left on the tool after use. An American, Lawrence Keely, published an article in 1977, deeming that it is possible to determine the use of a stone implement by observing its edge with a microscope. China should also do this.

Recently in China, radiocarbon absolute dating has been installed. Ancient geomagnetic determination has also been employed, along with other methods such as the fission determination method, the heat-release light method and the amino-acid reaction method, but the strides are not large enough. Many technical problems remain to be solved.

International academic exchanges and cooperation are important; for instance, the problem of the origin of mankind itself is an international problem. The problem can not be solved without international cooperation. The problem of ancient culture as well is no exception. Every country has its own culture, but they are not always locally born and bred; there must have been propagations and interchanges. Both European and Chinese fine stone implements have their generality and individuality. To get a clear understanding of these two systems is no easy task. That is a worthwhile topic for world researchers to make their mutual endeavour.

Sciences are developing. Due to the incessant new finds of human fossil remains, we will soon have a better understanding of human history. To enlarge his scope, one has to go up on a new height. Let us make our best effort together.

A Summary of Chinese Agricultural Archaeology

Chen Wenhua

Results of 35-year research are to be reviewed according to the archaeological data obtained in the course of time, in order to observe the Chinese agricultural scientific and technological developing history. As space is limited, it is impossible to enumerate all the materials; this just gives a brief overview of the findings.

(1) The New Stone Age

More than ten thousand years ago, having gathered wild plants as food for many years, men began to grasp the growing pattern of plants and cultivate their own food. That was the invention of agriculture. At that time men entered the New Stone Age.

The main technique was sowing and cropping with the hands. Later, stone and shell knives were used for cropping, and stone mills for grinding cereals. A small stone knife, 28,000 years old, has been unearthed at Zhiyu, Shuoxian County, Shanxi Province, from later period ruins of the Old Stone Age. A stone mill was found at Xiachuan, Qinshui County, Shanxi Province.

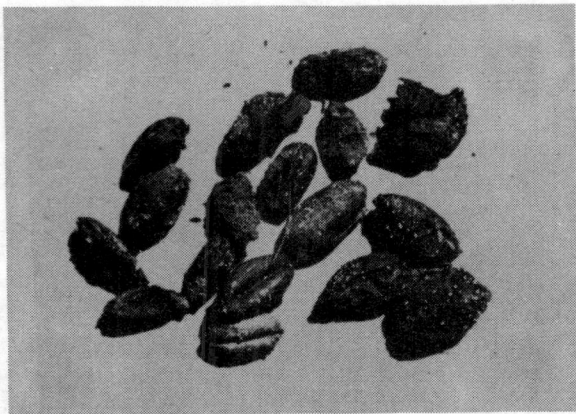

Wheat of the New Stone Age

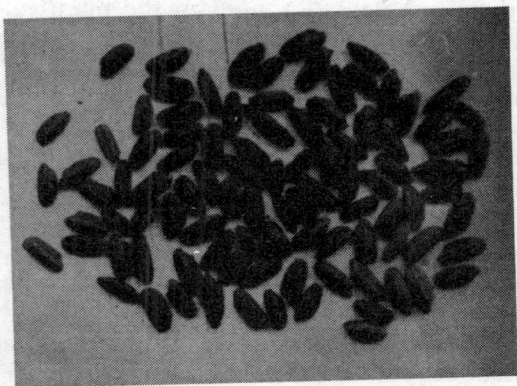

Paddy rice of the New Stone Age

The mill is made of sandstone, in the shape of a plate; the bottom has a natural surface while the surrounding rim was made by hitting. After repeated grinding, the central part has been hollowed out; evidently it was used for grinding cereals. When agriculture was first invented, these two kinds of farm tools were first developed. (In ruins of the New Stone Age, even of the Shang and Zhou dynasties, large amounts of stone, shell and ceramic knives and stone and shell sickles have been unearthed. Stone mills, too, have been found, but not many.)

Shortly after this, primitive men began to fell trees with stone axes and adzes and then set fire to burn grass on the land. This was called slash-and-burn cultivation, therefore stone axes and adzes were also regarded as farming tools. Further, men invented wooden spades to level land and make ditches, which is called spade-tilling (lei si 耒耜). *Lei* originated from the pointed-end wooden stick used in the plant-gathering period. A transverse bar is fitted above the sharp end of a stick for the foot to tread on in order to dig deeper; the bone or shell character was written as ⵝ. Later it developed two teeth, written as 大. But because it was made of wood, which is hard to preserve, very few have been discovered. In the New Stone Age ruins at Jiangzhai, Lintong County, Shaanxi Province and at Miaodigou, Shanxian County, Henan Province, both *lei* and *si* have been found. In the *Book of Change* (*Yi Jing*), a quotation says, "Shen Nong made *si* with wood." Because wood wore down easily, the scapula and slab were used. In past archaeological reports, the so-called stone plough and spade should be referred to as stone *si*. Those ruins at Peiligang and Cishan belonged to this phase of the age. In the ruins of Hemudu, Yuyao, Zhejiang Province, a large number of bone *si* and a few wooden *si* have been found. People are reminded that there are fewer finds of wooden tools because of easy decaying, particularly in those ruins. Only stone knives and sickles were found but very few stone *si* (spade) and hoes were unearthed. In the final analysis, such tools did exist during that period of time.

In those late period New Stone Age ruins, such as Songjiang of Shanghai; Qiansanyang, Wuxing of Zhejiang Province; Wuxian County of Jiangsu Province, etc., were also unearthed some stone ploughs and other soil-breaking tools, which indicate that ploughing originated very early in China. This is of great significance in the history of farming tools. At the time, ploughs must have been drawn by men; it is impossible that ploughs were pulled by cattle. Maybe paddy-field ploughing started first. At the time, deep tilling was still impossible.

The cultivation of millet and wheat along the Yellow River Basin and paddy rice along the Yangtse River, at least, has a history of seven to eight thousand years. Because millet is fast-growing with strong sprouts, able to endure drought, resist saline and alkali, and easier to cultivate than the cultivated-millet and wheat, it had been the main cereal in the loess plateau up to the Shang and Zhou dynasties. Carbonized millet has been found in the ruins of Hetaozhuang, Minhe, Qinghai Province; Jiangzhai, Lintong, Shaanxi Province; Dongkang, Ning'an, Heilongjiang Province; and Yantai, Shandong Province, totalling more than ten districts. Cultivated millet (*shu*, after husking called *xiao mi*) is derived from green bristlegrass, and has a history of more than 6,500 years. Later in the Cishan Ruins a large amount of *shu* ashes had been found, dating the history of *shu* (cultivated millet) back to more than 8,000 years. There are as many as 88 granary heaps, and storing caves may contain a hundred thousand *jin* of grain. So great is the figure that we have to reevaluate the productivity of primitive agriculture.

The origin of wheat was not in China, but the inscriptions of bone or shell have the word *mai* (wheat). In the past, grains of wheet of 3,000 years ago were unearthed only in the ruins of Balikun, Xinjiang Province, and grains of wheat of the Western Zhou Dynasty had been found at Diaoyutai, Haoxian County, Anhui Province. Recently, wheat of 4,000 years ago has been found at the upper reaches of the Kongque River in Xinjiang Province, putting back its history to the late period of the New Stone Age.

Paddy rice has been found in more than 20 ruins in the Yangtse River basin; those in the ruins of Luojiajiao, Tongxiang County, Zhejiang Province, and Hemudu, Yuyao, Zhejiang Province, have a history of more than 7,000 years. These finds prove that China is the earliest rice-cultivating country in the world. Finds from the ruins of Huanglianshu, Xichuan County; Yuxian County; Yangshaocun, Minchi County; Dahecun, Zhengzhou of Henan Province, Xixia County of Shandong Province and Guzhen County of Anhui Province on the basin of Yellow River and Huaihe River, also have a history of four or five thousand years.

In China, agriculture and husbandry simultaneously developed in ancient times. The earliest domesticated animals are horses, cattle, sheep, chickens, dogs and pigs. Remains of pigs have been found most often in the ruins. The notion that agriculture comes from husbandry is untrue, at least in China.

Silkworm raising was accomplished earliest in China; the find of half a silkworm cocoon from the Yangshao site 50 years ago was the evidence. Silk tatters and ribbons unearthed in 1950 from the ruins of Qianshanyang, Wuxing, Zhejiang Province, have been analysed to be silk of domesticated worms. Pottery unearthed at Meiyan, Wujiang, Jiangsu Province and Hemudu, has silkworm designs. Between the wild silkworm and home raising there is a history of at least four to five thousand years. *Yue Jue Shu* says Emperor Huangdi started the silk clothing industry and cultivated mulberry (for silkworms) and hemp;this is from historical records. Archaeological data also pointed out that vegetables like mustard, cabbage, gourd, etc., had also been raised.

From what we have stated above, we come to know the compilation of the history of primitive agriculture totally relies upon the materials of archaeology. One can well appreciate the great contribution agricultural archaeology has offered to history, particularly agricultural history.

(2) The Xia, Shang and Western Zhou Dynasties

During the Shang and Zhou periods, Chinese traditional agricultural technique was in the embryonic stage. Fragmentary literary materials can be consulted, but for better understanding a large amount of archaeological data has to be relied upon.

In that period, the farming production centre was on the loess plateau of the mid-upper reaches of the Yellow River, therefore the main crops were still the land-grown broomcorn millet (*shu*), the non-gluey millet (*ji*), the cultivated millet (*su*), wheat (*mai*), etc. In the inscriptions of bone or shell, the character for *shu* appeared more than 300 times, *ji* 40 times, *su* and *mai* rarely appeared. In the *Book of Songs* (*Shi Jing*), *shu* (28) and *ji* (10) appeared most often, but few real objects have been unearthed. Recently at Hanchuan, Hubei Province; Maojiazui, Qichun County, Hubei Province; and Jiaozhuang, Donghai County, Jiangsu Province, grains of nonglutinous rice of the Western Zhou Dynasty have been unearthed. Grains of wheat of 3,000 years ago have been found at Balikun, Xinjiang Province. Wheat grains have also been discovered at Diaoyutai, Haoxian County, Anhui Province. Ancient men even took seeds of hemp as food; those unearthed at Taixi, Haocheng, Hebei Province are of the Shang Dynasty. Beans of the Spring and Autumn Period have also been found at Yangtun, Yongqing County, Jilin Province. Beans have been mentioned in *Shi Jing*.

In this period farming tools did not make much progress, but people began to understand intertilling. Some smaller bronze tools had been invented for that purpose. Compared with bronze weapons and manual tools, farming tools were much fewer in number. Unearthed from the ruins of many places are a large amount of stone, bone, ram shell and wood farming tools. It is needless to emphasize the employment of bronze in farming production in that period of time.

Husbandry further developed in the Shang Dynasty. Words like pigpen, stable, sheep-fold, and pigsty had been coined among the inscriptions of bone or shell. Sacrificial horses, sheep, pigs and dogs have been found in the Shang and Zhou tombs at Anyang and Chang'an, etc. Ducks and geese had been raised; in the Shang Ruins a stone duck and jade goose have been unearthed. At the site of Fushan Orchard, Jurong County, Jiangsu Province, there is a pot of hen and duck eggs, similar to present sizes; fine varieties of poultry had been bred.

Jade, silkworms, and silk remnants had repeatedly appeared in tombs; characters like mulberry, silk, silk material, etc., also appeared among bone or shell inscriptions. But expensive silk materials were only for the ruling class; the vast number of slaves could only wear coarse linen clothes, therefore the cultivation of hemp was more developed. In the ruins of Taixi, Haocheng County, Hebei Province, linen has been discovered, which is a very rare artifact indeed.

(3) The Spring and Autumn Period and the Warring States

This period was the formative years of Chinese traditional agriculture, as well as the fast-developing epoch of farming tools. The rise of cattle tilling and iron tools marked a new era. Iron ploughshares have been unearthed at Huixian County, Henan Province; Yixian and Wu'an of Hebei; Linzi and Tengxian of Shandong; Lantian and Xi'an of Shaanxi; Houma of Shanxi and Inner Mongolia, illustrating that cattle tilling was popular in the Central Plains. Iron tools appeared in the later decades of the Spring and Autumn Period. In the No. 314 Tomb, Shiziling, Changsha, Hunan, was unearthed a small iron spade and in the Cement Member Plant, Luoyang, Henan, was unearthed another spade; they are the earliest iron farming tools ever discovered. Before mid- and late-Warring States most tools were wood, stone, bone, shell and a few bronze; after that time, iron tools increased.

From a batch of farming tool casting moulds unearthed at Xinglong, Hebei, we can see the productivity was large, which confirms the establishment of the feudalistic relations between production and the

Bronze toothed sickles of the Spring and Autumn Period and the Warring States

rapid growth of farming. A wooden spade with iron-edged double feeth was unearthed at Jinancheng, Jiangling, Hubei; it is the earliest wooden spade artifact. It not only lets us see how it looks, but also makes us understand that the small spades unearthed in the past were actually linked with the wooden shafts and then used. In recent years, many bronze tools have been unearthed at Liuhe and Suzhou of Jiangsu; Shucheng and Guichi of Anhui; Jiangling and Xiangyang of Hubei; Jiangxi; Yunnan, etc. This reminds us that when iron tools were already widely used, bronze was still employed in some of the southern provinces.

During the Warring States, husbandry and silkworm breeding were more stressed. *Guan Zi* pointed out, "When five cereals are cropped, people have enough food; when raising mulberry, hemp and six livestock-and-poultry, people get rich." From the designs on the bronze pots and from the fine silk-weaving materials unearthed at Sichuan, Henan, Hubei, Hunan, etc., we can see mulberry farmers had bred new varieties of low-trunk type mulberries, in order to increase their productivity. That was six hundred years earlier than the records about the ground-mulberry noted in *Qi Min Yao Shu* (*The Manual of Important Arts for the People*). The livestock moulds unearthed at Hubei and Yunnan are the real object evidence of Mo Zi's "All of the cereal croppers are raising livestock." Mules had been crossbred between horses and donkeys to procure the good qualities of both animals. Two mules on a sculptured bronze ornament found at Kesengzhuang, Chang'an, Shaanxi, witnessed that mules had been brought forth among the northern minorities, which was an immense accomplishment in the world history of husbandry.

Gardening had been divided from field cropping; more than twenty kinds of vegetables like melon, gourd, chives, sunflower, celery, ginger, etc., and over twenty kinds of fruit trees like peach, apricot, plum, *mei* (another kind of plum), jujube, chestnut, etc., had been planted. In tombs of Hubei, Hunan, Henan, and Guangdong, gourds and fruits often appeared. Jujube and chestnut contain ample protein and fat, so could be stored for a long time and used as staple foods. In the Warring States tombs, jujube and chestnut were often used as burial articles.

(4) The Han Dynasty

Archaeological finds of the Han Dynasty are plentiful and contain an immense number of farming relics, especially those portrait bricks, portrait stone carvings, frescoes, farming and irrigation models which are valuable image data in the study of farming techniques of that period of time. Zhao Guo of the Western Han propelled the shift-tilling method to have the field furrow irrigated; so doing promoted production. But so far there is a lack of evidence as to how the field actually looked. A farmland model unearthed in Mianxian, Shaanxi Province, shows a pool of water to the left and a furrowed field on the right, something like the ridge culture of the Han Dynasty. In Yuzhuang, Huaiyang, Henan, a pottery manor model was unearthed, with a courtyard on the right and an enclosing wall on the left. Within the wall is a water well, beside which are rows of rectangular ridged pieces of land in a field. It must be a vegetable garden model, from which we would have a better understanding of the shift-tilling method of the Han Dynasty.

From Pinglu, Shanxi; Mizi, Shaanxi; Helinge'er, Inner Mongolia; Tengxian, Shandong; and Suining, Jiangsu, were unearthed stone portraits of cattle tilling; the finds show that cattle tilling was popular in various places. Models of wooden ploughshares have been discovered at Wuwei, Gansu Province—the double cattle pole-carrying type and the single-drawn type; both designs had been finalized in the Han Dynasty. The find of an iron ploughshare wall of the Western Han Dynasty from Xianyang, Shaanxi, demonstrates

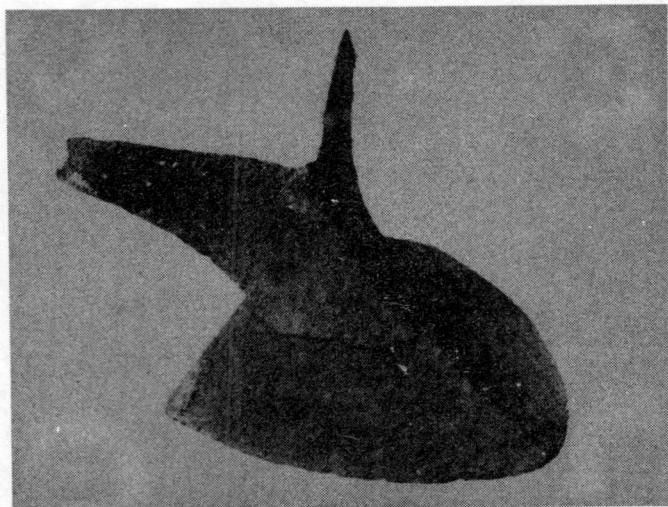

Iron mouldboard and ploughshare of
the Western Han Dynasty

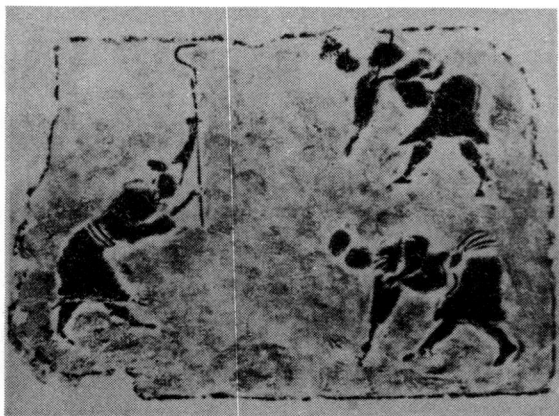

Sowing picture of brick carving
of the Eastern Han Dynasty

the existence of soil turning and crushing, a thousand years earlier than in the West. From the portrait bricks and stones, murals and models unearthed in Sichuan, Shanxi, Henan and Shandong, we recognize the construction of a drill barrow, a treadle huller, a winnowing cart and millstones. These help us understand how they did the soil preparing, seeding, intertilling, collecting manure, irrigating, cropping, etc.

Iron tools had been widely used. From many places have been unearthed toothed spades, small spades, double-shared ploughs, picks, spades, pickaxes, multi-toothed picks, sickles, etc. Pottery figurines holding spades or picks, unearthed in Sichuan and Henan, show us how the Han farmers handled farming tools and how the wooden shafts were fitted. Iron spades were the most generally used digging tools of the time. In

"On Ditchs and Canals" of the *Han Shu* (*History of the Han Dynasty*), there is the description, "...numerous spades are raised to make clouds (scattering the soil)." In No. 3 Tomb of Mawangdui, Changsha, Hunan Province, was unearthed a whole spade, from which we could see its true features.

Crops of the Han Dynasty that have been discovered in tombs are as follows: cereals—millet, wheat, oats, broomcorn millet, non-glutinous millet, beans, red beans, hemp seeds, rice, sorghum, job's-tears; vegetables—gourd, turnip, lotus root, ginger, red pepper, celery, mustard, winter mallow, taro, bamboo shoots, cucumber; melons and fruits—sweet melon, jujube, chestnut, apricot, different kinds of plum, walnut, persimmon, oranges, grapefruit, red bayberry, loquat, olive, litchi. These are valuable real-object data in the research of the farming crops of the Han Dynasty, which reflect the prosperity of cropping and gardening at that time.

The development of an agricultural economy promoted the flourishing of husbandry. Cattle and horses are the motive power of military affairs, communications and cultivation; particularly horses are regarded as the origin of military equipment. Horse raising was highly developed; from the pottery, bronze and wooden horse burials we can see the elegant varieties of horses of the time. *Shi Ji Ping Zhun Shu* (*On the Balance of Taxation*) says: "There were horses in the streets of the multitude and flocks of them among the criss-cross footpaths of the fields."

Because cattle tilling had been popular, of course much attention was devoted to cattle raising. On Qin bamboo slips, unearthed at Shuihudi, Yunmeng, Hubei

Province, there is *Jiu Yuan Lü* (*Law of Cattle Breeding*) which calls cattle used for tilling "field-cattle", and there are stipulations that certain breeds are prized. That was the earliest law of animal husbandry in the world. The Qin and Han governments laid much stress on tilling cattle, therefore pottery cattle, wooden cattle and images of cattle-tilling have been repeatedly unearthed from the Han tombs of different localities. In the Han tomb of Lanshi, Foshan, Guangdong, there is a pottery cow licking its young by turning back its head, which is a portrayal of cattle breeding of the Han Dynasty. The stone portrait of cattle castration unearthed from an Eastern Han tomb at Nanyang District of Henan Province, up to now is the only image relating to the technique of cattle castration of the Han Dynasty, a valuable reference in the study of Chinese husbandry veterinary history.

Cattle and horses were employed for their dynamic strength; but of meat-producing animals, such as pigs, sheep, chickens, ducks and other smaller animals, many pottery models have been unearthed from different places. From the models we can see the fine varieties of animals. Some of them are exactly like they are today; evidently there is a direct line of descent. In the Han dynasty, pigs were raised in sties in order to collect manure for fertilizing the fields. The unearthed pigsty models are often connected with human latrines as a whole body, the excrement to feed the pigs and the pig feces to fertilize the soil. Some rural villages are still like this.

Moreover, the brick portraits of mulberry gardens, the stone carvings of mulberry plucking, the stone portraits of silk spinning and weaving, and the silk fabrics unearthed at Sichuan, Shandong, Jiangsu, and Hunan, also have significant scientific value in the research of the sericultural history of the Han Dynasty.

(5) The Kingdom of Wei, the Jin Dynasty and the Northern and Southern Dynasties

Aside from the iron tools and animal models, the brick farming portraits unearthed at Jiayuguan and Jiuquan of Gansu Province are important finds for the agricultural archaeology of that period. *Qi Min Yao Shu* was published during this period, from which we can understand the farming techniques of the time. The murals of Jiayuguan afforded us large amount of image data, such as portraits of cattle-tilling, soil raking, soil loosening, seed sowing, winnowing, flail threshing, mulberry plucking, herding, pig feeding, well-water drinking, etc., not only give us a vivid sight of farming and husbandry of the time but also set out a hundred years earlier what is noted in *Qi Min Yao Shu*. The soil-raking model of a Western Jin tomb, Lianxian, Guangdong, and the soil-raking model of the Southern Dynasty tomb at Daoshui, Wuzhou, Guangxi, give us the stereoimage of the field-levelling tools, which is of great scientific value.

In 1975 at Mianchi, Henan, a batch of cellar stored iron tools and moulds of the Kingdom of Wei were unearthed. The farm tools contained are ploughs, ploughshares, spades, hoes, pitchforks, sickles, and drills of different sizes; they are worn scrap iron for smelting. We can see iron farm tools in this period were much more advanced and popular than in the Han

Dynasty. These are also important gains of the agricultural archaeology of the time.

(6) The Tang, Song, Yuan and Ming Dynasties

Since the Tang and Song, agricultural books have been published more and more. However, agricultural archaeology still has obtained no mean results; many iron farm implements of the Tang and Song have been discovered in Henan, Hebei, Shandong, Jiangsu and Jiangxi provinces. In Heilongjiang, Jilin, Liaoning and Beijing, iron farming tools of the Liao, Kin and Yuan dynasties have also been found, which are of great significance in the study of the agricultural productivity of the North in that period.

The great invention of the Tang Dynasty was the curved-shaft ploughshare, which was described in Lu Guimeng's *Lei Si Jing*. But when it took the place of the long-shaft plough is still unknown. From the mural portrait of cattle-stilling unearthed in Li Shou's Tomb, Sanyuan, Shaanxi, and from the frescoes of No. 445 Dunhuang Caves, Gansu Province, we can see that though the ploughshares are still of double-cattle pole-bearing type, yet the shafts are long-curved ones. They must be an interim type between the long straight shafts and the short curved ones. It is thus clear that the real curved-shaft ploughshares must have appeared during the middle and late Tang. Moreover, in the Caves there are still a few portraits of tilling of the Song Dynasty; these, added to the frescoes of Yanshang Monastery, and Song and Yuan paintings, are the image materials in the research of the agricultural production of the Song Dynasty, making up for any missing information in farming books.

The period after the Ming and Qing is no focal point of archaeology, therefore few farming relics have been discovered; but in museums of various places many farming tools have been collected. In some of the Ming tombs, real objects of grains and fruits have been excavated, which are of value in research of the history of some of the varieties of the modern crops. At the same time, long handed-down stone carvings and paintings such as Lou Shou's *Geng Zhi Tu* (*Portraits of Farming and Weaving*), Fang Guancheng's *Mian Hua Tu* (*Portrait of Cotton*), stone carvings of the Qing Dynasty and painting scrolls of Jiao Bingzhen, are all valuable relics for research work.

Archaeological finds in this aspect of research are not small in number. Compared with that of foreign countries, ours has its own features; we have studied not only the origin of agriculture and the development of primitive farming, but also the formation and development of the traditional agriculture, from which we have obtained a handsome result.

Recent Important Finds in Chinese Archaeology

Yang Hong

(1) Fossil Remains of Lantian Man (found 1963)

In 1963 at Chenjiawo Village, Lantian County, Shaanxi Province, there was unearthed a lower jaw fossil of an upright standing man. In 1964 at Gongwangling, Lantian County, a tooth and later a skull were also discovered. The skull comprises a complete jawbone, the right side temporal bone and the upper jaw, on which are the second and third molars, part of the left side upper jaw and a large part of the nose bone. The earlier excavated tooth was the left upper second molar belonging to the same skeleton, probably a thirty-or-more-year-old female. The skeleton was named as a sub-breed of the upright-standing Lantian Man, or generally called Lantian Man. The skull has many primitive characteristics: the eyebrowridges are broad and strong, the forehead low and flat, the skull is very thick, and the brain capacity is about 780 ml., smaller than that of the Peking Man. The site at Gongwangling belongs to the early stage of the Miocene epoch, palaeo-magneto-determination dated a million years old, or 750-800 thousand years earlier than the Peking Man. In the same stratum were also unearthed some sharp pointed triangular stone tools, comprising chopping-and-hacking tools, scrapers and stone balls, small rocks and slabs; all are very crude. Three or four heaps of ashes and charcoal slags were also unearthed, which may be evidence of fire use. The fossil from Chenjiawo is an old female, more akin to the Peking Man, magneto-determined 500,000 or 650,000 years old, which is later than that from Gongwangling. Some call it the sub-breed Chenjiawo upright standing man, or the Chenjiawo Man, while Lantian Man alone refers to the fossil from Gongwangling.

(2) Fossil Remains of Yuanmou Man (discovered 1965)

The earliest upright-standing man's fossils so far discovered in China are the two frontteeth of Yuanmou Man found at Shangnabeng, Yuanmou County, Yunnan Province. In the same site were also unearthed 29 varieties of mammals such as Nihewan sabre-toothed tiger (Megantereon nihawanensis), hyena (Hyena licenti), Yunnan horse (Equns yunnanensis), Nestorithe rium sp., Chinese rhinoceros (Rhinoceros sinensis), Axis shansius, etc. According to animal fossils and spore tests, the surroundings where the Yuanmou Man lived must have been a forest grassland and cooler than it is now. A large quantity of charcoal slags and two pieces of burnt bones have also been discovered. Both teeth discovered are the incisors, one left and one right, belonging to the same adult. It has been nominated as Homo erectus yuanmouensis, generally called the Yuanmou Man, who lived 1,700,000 years ago, and possibly knew how to use fire.

(3) The Ruins of Cishan (excavated 1976-78)

In probing the early stage of culture of the New Stone Age in North China, the discovery of the Cishan Ruins is of great importance. The site is on the table-land of the north bank of Minghe River to the southwest of Wu'an County, Hebei Province; house-foundations, cellar-caves and large amount of relics have been found, carbon dated to 5,400-5,100 B.C. and named the Cishan Culture. There are not many house-foundations, most are semi-ground-cave type construc-tions, in round or oval cross-section. There are 468 caves of oblong, round, oval or irregular shapes; most are oblong. Some of the caves are heaped with decayed grains—maybe a kind of millet. The stone farming tools unearthed are knives, sickles, hatchets, spades and millstones for cereal grinding. The shape of the millstone is quite unique-something like a willow leaf, with feet under the bottom. Also unearthed are bone arrowheads, fishdarts, shuttles for knitting nets, and other tools for hunting and fishing, as well as skeletons of birds, animals and aquatic animals, which shows the farming economy had arrived at a certain level. Daily used pottery is crude and typically handmade, with a low kiln temperature, simple in shape and design, signifying that handicrafts were still low.

After the discovery of the Cishan Culture, another

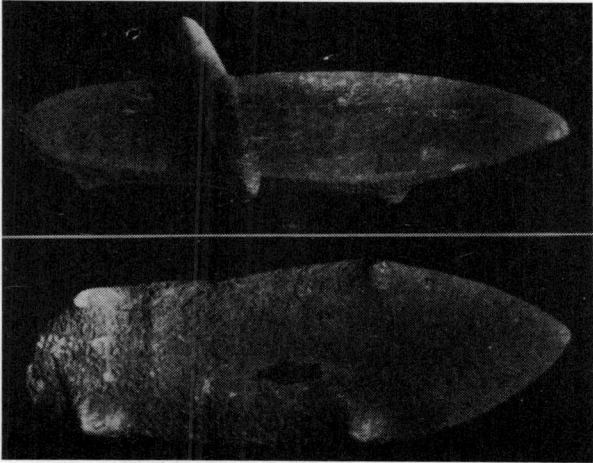

Millstone and milling rod unearthed from the Cishan Site

site of the same epoch was unearthed at Peiligang, Xinzheng County, Henan Province, which has been called the Peiligang Culture. The two cultures are close to each other, but each has its own features. Some call them the Cishan-Peiligang Culture. Those works have made a considerable breakthrough in the research of the early stage of culture of the New Stone Age at the middle reaches of the Yellow River.

(4) The Banpo Ruins (excavated 1954-57)

The excavation of the Banpo site was the first large-scale exposure of the compact community vestiges of a primitive society since the founding of New China. The site is in the Banpo Village on the east bank of Chanhe River, 6 kilometres to the east of Xi'an, Shaanxi Province. From a total area of 50,000 square metres, 10,000 square metres were unearthed. Excavated were 46 houses, 200 caves, 2 sties, 2 kilns, 250 tombs and a large amount of relics of Banpo type of the Yangshao Culture. The primitive community lived in a circle; in the centre were semi-ground caves and houses of square or round shape. Houses were built on two stretches of land, each with a big house for public gathering. Surrounding are smaller houses, near which are storing caves and animal folds. According to the custom of the time,

Scene of the excavation of the Banpo Site

children's urns were buried within the circle. Around the whole dwelling area there is a defending ditch, 5.6 metres wide and 5 metres deep. Beyond the ditch to the east side are the kilns; to the north is the burial ground for the clan. More than a hundred tombs have been excavated. Most are single tombs; only two were co-burials—one contains two man, the other, four children, which may reflect the burial custom of the matriarchal society. Burial articles are mostly pottery and bone or pearl ornaments. Among the finds there are fine clay and coarse red pottery vessels, farming, fishing and hunting tools as well as ornaments made of stone, bone, horn or pottery.

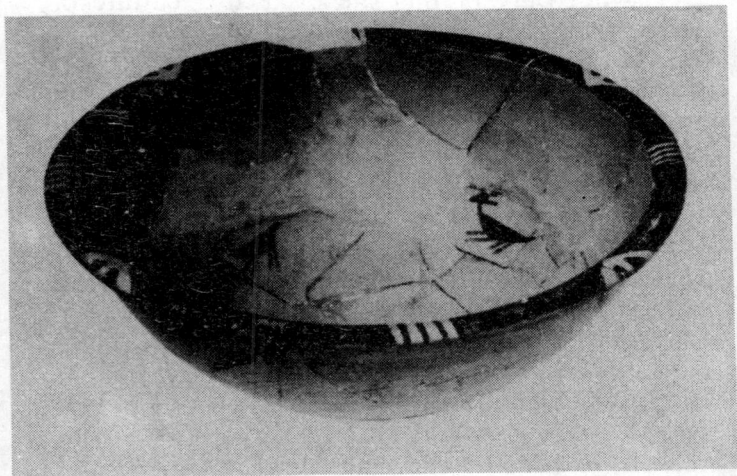

Deer-designed pottery basin unearthed
from the Banpo Site

Some of the pottery is coloured and beautifully designed; apart from geometrical patterns, there are also human masks, fish, deer, plants and other designs from life, precious objects of remote ancient arts. On the tapes along the mouth or bottom of pottery bowls, 22 different symbols have been discovered; maybe that was the beginning of ancient characters.

(5) The Ruins of Hemudu (excavated 1973-74, 1977-78)

The discovery of this site exposed a culture of the New Stone Age on the lower reaches of the Yangtse River, carbon dated 5,000—3,300 B.C. It also extended the sphere of our archaeological research in the New Stone Age and further pointed out that cultures on the reaches of both the Yangtse and Yellow rivers flourished simultaneously. Hemudu is in Yuyao County, Zhejiang Province; after two excavations, an area of 2,600 square metres has been exposed. Remnants of paddy, criss-cross buildings, bone spades, wooden tools and charcoal-mottled black pottery have been found. The pottery is crude, mainly charcoal-mottled black and sand-mottled red, as well as red-coated. Most are flat-bottomed or round-bottomed vessels, such as cauldrons, pots, bowls with a handle, *he* (a tall vessel with 3 feet and a lid) and fire-supports. Supports and cauldrons were the main utensils used in cooking during the period of Hemudu Culture. In the ruins, remnants of rice paddy are

Scene of the second excavation of the Hemudu Site

quite common, with the heaping layer as thick as over a metre, abundant and well preserved; among the New Stone Age archaeological finds this is an unparalleled discovery. In probing the origin of rice planting, this is of great significance. About a hundred bone spades, wooden spades, bored stone hatchets, double-holed stone knives and huge wooden pestles for husking rice have been unearthed, which shows the advances of farming production. Livestock raising was mainly confined to dogs and pigs; remnants of pig bones and teeth are scattered everywhere. There is also a pottery pig model. On the outer wall of a pottery basin there are carved ears of rice and an image of a pig. Hunting and fishing too occupied a certain place in the social economy, which assumption is justified by the finds of a large amount of wild animal bones.

(6) The Tomb Sites of Dawenkou (excavated 1959)

A graveyard of the New Stone Age has been found on both banks of the Dawen River at Dawenkou Town, Taian County, Shandong Province. In 1959, more than a hundred graves were excavated; owing to the unique cultural features, the spot has been named the Dawenkou Culture; epoch from around 3,500-2,500 B.C. All of the graves are oblong earth pits, very few of them have the traces of wood burial. In most graves, one person is buried; but there are 8 graves in which two or three are buried. Burial objects are mainly pottery utensils and stone implements, jade, bone, horn, and shell wares as well as exquisite hollow carved ivory combs, tube-shaped objects, *zong* (a section of tube with a circular inside and octagonal outside), etc. In some of the graves, there seems to have been a custom of putting river deer's teeth and tortoise shell into the grave. In 43 graves, 96 pieces of pig skulls and lower jaws have been found; they might be the symbols of private property.

One thing worth attention is that the sizes of funeral vary a great deel into three types—big, medium and small, according to the size of graves and the amount of burial objects. Some of the small graves only contain the body and no burials at all, while the large graves are full of beautiful pottery, jade and ivory wares from scores up to a hundred pieces, indicating that the poor and rich had been divided. At the same time, the finds of this graveyard have afforded important data in the research of the history of Chinese remote patriachal society.

Tomb No. 35 of the Dawenkou Graves

(7) The Ruins of Taosi (excavated since 1978)

This is an important site of the Longshan Culture excavated in 1978 at the south of Taosi Village, Xiangfen County, Shanxi Province. It has a total area of about 3,000,000 square metres, scattered with habitation ruins and tombyards. Many small dwellings have been found, and can be divided into three types: houses built above the ground, semi-ground caves and caves below ground surface. Around the houses are streets, water-wells, pottery kilns, cellar caves, etc. A limekiln and its storing caves have also been found, showing that lime had been employed in buildings.

To the southeast of the dwelling site is the tomb-yard, in which more than one thousand graves have been unearthed so far; all are vertical earth pits in oblong shape. Graves are divided into three categories: big, medium and small, which differ greatly. Burial objects vary a good deal: in big tombs there are wooden coffins, as many as one or two hundred pieces of coloured pottery and colour-painted wooden wares, particularly the cylindrical big wooden drum as tall as a metre, capped with crocodile skin on the top, which has been unearthed together with huge stone chimes; these might mark the status of the dead. Aside from these, there are also sacrificial objects and ornaments such as *zong*, *yuan*, and *huan* (ring) made of jade or stone. Complete sets of pig skeletons have also been unearthed. All the dead are males; it is presumed that they were the actual chieftains of tribes and social wealth had fallen into their hands.

In medium graves, wooden coffins were used and accompanied with several up to scores of burials—such as sets of pottery and stone or jade wares. Sometimes the lower jaws of pigs are also found in these graves. Most owners of the graves are males; only in the medium graves among the flanks of the big tombs are some of the owners females. Small graves cover 90 percent of the total number of graves. They have no coffin, nor any burial objects, thus forming a sharp contrast with the big graves and exposing the division between the poor and the rich. There must have been class differences among the tribes; the embryo of a nation might have been formed.

Another thing worth mentioning is that aside from the pottery and stone implements, a small copper bell has been found, which shows that copper had appeared at the time. On a coloured pottery plate there is a coiled dragon, which is the oldest dragon design ever discovered in the Central Regions; it must be the mark of a certain tribe, carbon 14 dated 2,500-1,900 B.C., corresponding to the Xia Dynasty and within the boundary of the Xia Dynasty ruins. Therefore further excavation and research of the ruins of Taosi is of importance in solving the outstanding problem of the Xia Culture; at the same time, the finds also provide valuable data in restoring the history of Chinese ancient classes and the birth of the state.

(8) The Ruins of Changdu Karuo (excavated 1978-79)

This is the first excavation of ruins of the Stone Age in Tibet, situated in Karuo Village, Jiaka District, 12 kilometres to the southeast of Changdu City. Scores of house bases of different constructions have been discovered; some were built on the ground, while some are rectangular semi-ground caves. Some of the semi-ground caves are surrounded by pebble walls as tall as a metre, pointed by yellow mud. Unearthed are stone, bone or pottery implements; most stone tools were chipped. They consist of big or small scrapers and beating tools, as well as many fine tools such as awls, prism- and flat-shaped small stones and stone-leaves. Only a few ground tools were found, for example, hatchets, adzes, chisels, arrow-heads and stone boring knives. Pottery was made of coarse sand, very few of fine clay; most are grey or red in colour, and adorned with various rope-patterned and fine-stacked designs. Very little coloured pottery has been found; mostly they are small, flat-bottomed pots, basins and bowls. Farming production might have been engaged in because remnants of millet have been found. Bones of pigs and cattle might belong to domestic animals. The finds of skeletons of birds and animals show that hunting was important in the economic life of the time. One thing worth attention is that the site is near the river of Lancangjiang and its sub-streams, but no fishing tools nor any fish bones have been found; this shows that the inhabitants didn't use fish as food. The excavation of these ruins exposes the culture of east Tibet in the Stone Age, a good start in probing the primitive culture and the social life of these regions.

(9) The Ruins of Yanshi Erlitou (excavated 1959)

Exploring the history of the Xia Dynasty, Mr Xu Xusheng discovered the site of these ruins at Erlitou Village, Yanshi County, Henan Province. The north end of the site is along the Luohe River, covering an area of 3 square kilometres. The excavation was conducted to the depth of 3-4 metres. The cultural stratum could be divided into four continuous stages, named the Erlitou Culture, carbon 14 determined 1,900-1,500 B.C., which continued for 400 years. The excavation had been continued for more than thirty years beginning in 1959. Many cultural remnants have been found, which mainly belong to the third stage: a layout of a palace, general houses, pottery kilns, cellar caves and tomb burials. Two large ram-earthed palace sites have been found; No. 1 Foundation is 108 x 100 metres, with blanks for doors. To the north of the centre is a rectangular palace with pits of column bases still ranged in good order. If the palace were being restored, it would be 8 rooms wide and 3 rooms deep. To its northeast is No. 2 Foundation, similar to No. 1; ceramic drainage pipelines have been found at its east veranda. Grey pottery, stone and bone tools, jade sacrificial objects and ornaments, lacquer wares, and divining bones have been discovered; but what attracts people's attention are the bronzes—implements, weapons, vessels, musical instruments and ornaments. All the articles—*jue, jia* (drinking vessels), *ge* (dagger-axe), *qi* (axe) and *zu* (arrow-head)—are the earliest of their kinds so far unearthed, and of importance in the research of the metallurgical history of ancient China. However, on the nature of the Erlitou Culture, archaeologists have different opinions. Some opine that the site was a metropolis of the late period of the Xia Dynasty; others hold that the first and second stages belong to the Xia Culture while the third and fourth stages are only the vestiges of the early Shang Dynasty. Nevertheless, everyone believes the finding of these ruins renders significant help in probing the culture of the Xia Dynasty.

(10) Huangpi, Panlongcheng—a City Site of the Shang Dynasty (excavated 1974, 1976)

The discovery of a city site of the Shang Dynasty (1500 B.C.) in south China helps us understand the distribution of the Shang Culture and the nature of the city. The site is in Huangpi County, 5 kilometres to the north of Wuhan City, Hubei Province. To its south is the Fuhe River which flows into the Yangtse River and to the north is a small hillock. The city is somewhat square in shape, 290 metres from south to north and 260 metres east to west. Rammed earth remnants 1-3 metres tall still exist only on the south and west walls. Around the city is a ditch 14 metres wide and 4 metres deep. On the northeast highland inside the city are the remains of three palaces arranged in a row from front to back. The palaces face south; bases of columns and walls are still well preserved. Around the city are the

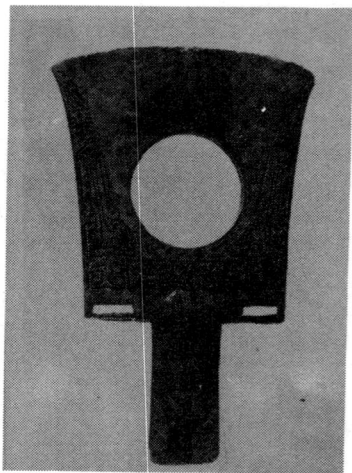

Bronze battle-axe unearthed from the site of Panlongcheng at Huangpi, Hubei Province

dwelling areas of the general inhabitants and the areas of the handicraft industry.

Graves have been found, those of the nobles concentrated in the parts of Lijiazui. In the large vertical earth pits, inner and finely-carved outer coffins were placed. There are human sacrifices buried together with the owners of graves. Burial objects are bronzes, pottery and jade wares in large quantity. In some tombs, the number of bronzes is up to scores; a huge battle-axe was found, which was used to denote the rank of the dead. But in nobles' smaller graves at Louziwan, only dogs and a small amount of bronzes have been found. In the vicinity of Yangjiawan, graves of the common people were unearthed; they are very small, coffined but with no outer coffin. Some of the graves were buried with a dog or a few pieces of pottery, or occasionally a small piece of bronze. Through intense investigation on the culture of the site, we know that there must have been a big state established by the Shang people on the reaches of the Yangtse River.

(11) Fuhao Tomb in the Yin Dynasty Ruins (excavated 1976)

A big tomb of the late period of the Shang Dynasty was excavated at the northwest of Xiaotun Village, Anyang City, Henan Province. In an oblong, 5.6 metres long, vertical earth pit were placed an inner coffin, an outer coffin and a large amount of exquisite burials-wares of bronze, jade, bone, ivory and pottery, as many as 1,928 pieces, added with 16 human sacrifices and 6 dogs. The upper part of the coffin-chamber is a rammed earth foundation of a house; column bases and foundation stones are still visible, denoting that above the grave there might have been a building for sacrifice. Some of the bronzes are inscribed with "Fuhao" or "Si Mu Xin". According to the inscriptions on bones or shells, Fuhao was a consort of King Wu Ding. So far this is the only grave of the Shang Dynasty whose status and date have been determined by the inscriptions on bones or shells. Among the bronzes are a set of three food steamers (*yan*); a pair of square wine vessels (*yi*) with lids in the shape of a palace; an owl-shaped wine vessel (*zun*); 4-footed wine vessels (*huang*); big battle-axes (*yue*), etc. Aside from sacrificial articles, wine vessels, cooking utensils, weapons, etc., there is a 4-sided knobbed round mirror. There are over 750 pieces of jade and precious stone wares; they are sacrificial objects, ceremonial articles and articles of everyday use. Many jade objects are carved into the shapes of human beings and animals; the brilliant artifice of dragons, phoenixes, strange birds and animals shows the high level of jade making of the time. Apart from these, also unearthed were three whole-tusk big ivory cups, fully carved and inlaid with turquoise; these also are rare artifacts of the Shang Dynasty.

(12) Zhouyuan Ruins (excavated since 1976)

The site is at the north of Qishan and Fufeng counties, Shaanxi Province, the birth place of the Zhou Dynasty before the end of the Shang Dynasty, and has a total area of about 15 square kilometres. So far, building foundations have been found at Fengchu, Qishan County and at Shaochen, Fufeng County. The building foundation at Fengchu is on a rammed earth base, 32.5 metres east to west, 43.5 metres south to north, and 1.5 metres high. The whole ground is partitioned into two symmetric closed courtyards, comprised of the gateway, front hall, back hall and the east and west wing rooms, linked by winding corridors, and with pottery- or pebble-laid drainage pipelines. The front hall is 17.2 metres long east to west, 6.1 metres wide north to south, with respectively 7 and 4 rows of regularly ranged column pits. From a cellar-cave in the west flank rooms, 17,000 pieces of divining bones and shells have been unearthed, among which were more than 200 miniaturely inscribed; the quantity of finds excels any of the previous finds in Shanxi, Shaanxi or Beijing, etc. The finds not only enrich our knowledge of the Western Zhou's characters but also afford valuable reference in the study of the history of the epoch.

Fifteen of the large-scale building foundations at Shaochen have been excavated, some of them well preserved. Most are over 20 metres long and 10-15 metres wide; column bases are well retained on the rammed-earth base. Because flat, tubular or eaves tiles often appeared, the big buildings must have been tile-roofed. Remains of workshops of bronze casting, bone, pottery and jade works have also been discovered.

At Hejia, Qishan County, and Qijia and Zhuang-bai, Fufeng County, many medium and small Zhou graves have been unearthed in rectangular vertical pits, accompanied by burials of fine bronzes and characteristic pottery, among which the bronzes from Bo Dong's tomb at Zhuangbai are most important. The story of how Bo Dong chased his adversary Tan Rong in the battlefield had been inscribed on some of the 14 bronzes unearthed. Because of the invasion of the Quan Rong tribes, the aristocracy ran away in a hurry; lots of cellar storage of bronzes were left in the original place. Since the 1950's, batches of the storage at Zhouyuan have been unearthed. Among them, important finds are the 37 pieces from Dongjia, Qishan County and the 103 pieces of the Wei Family from Zhuangbai of Fufeng County.

(13) City Site and Tombs of the Western Zhou at Liulihe (excavated since 1975)

This is an important ancient ruin for the study of the early cities of the Yan State. The site is situated on the highland 1.5 kilometres to the north of Liulihe Town, Fangshan County, Beijing, near Dongjialin Village. Graveyards are scattered outside the city; the aristocrats' graves in parts of Huangtupo to the southeast of the city are the most attractive. The excavation work is ongoing. The north wall is 829 metres long, and east and west walls have been found to the length of 300 metres. The foot of walls was built by rammed earth, about 10 metres thick. Outside around the city are ditches, while there are residences inside the city. Two hundred graves at Huangtupo have been excavated, including big, medium and small graves, and burials of chariots and horses. Some of the graves were buried with human sacrifices—one or two persons, mostly boys and girls. The burials unearthed comprise

Scene of the excavation of the Grave 1 chariots
and horses pit at Liulihe

bronzes, potteries, primitive porcelains, jade and precious stone wares, lacquer wares, cowries, etc. Particularly the wooden-based lacquer articles were in large number, some of them inlaid with mother-of-pearl into exquisite designs, made after the shapes of *dou* (bean), *hu* (melon) *lei*, *hu* (pot), *jiu* (bamboo-knitted grain container), cups, plates, *zu* (sacrificial utensil), *yi* (wine vessel), etc., giving us a new knowledge about the artistic level of lacquer-making in the Western Zhou period. Some of the bronzes—sacrificial vessels, weapons, chariots and horses which were beautifully made, are inscribed with "Yan Hou" ("匽侯 ," Marquis of

Yan), 匽 is the old way of character writing, which stands for 燕 ; these are all significant data for the reserach of the history of the Yan State.

(14) Marquis Yi's Tomb of Zeng (excavated 1978)

Aside from the beautiful tuned chime bells, other musical instruments, sacrificial articles, chariots and horses, attire, etc., have also been unearthed from the tomb of the Marquis Yi of Zeng up to more than ten thousand pieces; such an immense number was never before discovered in the history of excavation. The tomb is at Leigudun, the west suburbs of Suizhou City, Hubei Province, in a vertical rock pit. The whole grave was partitioned into four chambers, with the coffin in the east chamber. The coffin was made in two layers; the outer coffin was piled up by 171 square logs, bronze framed, red-lacquered inside and black-lacquered outside with red and yellow designs; the inner coffin was painted with vermilion lacquer and yellow- and black-designed, at two sides there are painted doors which are guarded by human-shaped holy animals holding halberds in hands. The dead body was wrapped in silk fabrics, but has decayed, only remnants are left. The skeleton still exists, around which 300 burials of jade and gold are placed. In the east and west chambers there are 21 human sacrifices, each has its own coffin and is accompanied with a small amount of jade wares and wooden combs. The skeleton has been determined to be from a male of 45 years old while all of the sacrifices are females of 13-25

The excavation of chime bells
of the Marquis Yi of Zeng

years old. By the side of the grave owner, there is a
coffin, in which is a dog. As well as the famous chime
bells, of musical instruments alone were unearthed 124
pieces: series *qing* (chime), drums, *se* (zither), *qin*
(seven-stringed zither), *sheng* (a cluster of reed pipes),
paixiao (a cluster of vertical bamboo flutes), *chi* (bamboo wind), etc., rendering valuable data for the research of Chinese musical history. Among the bronzes,
the huge *fou* weighs more than 300 kilograms; the set
of square *jian* and *hu* (used as an ice-box) are rare
articles. Among the lacquer wares, there are a coiled-
deer plate, a mandarin duck box, *dou* (stemmed vessel

with lid) and a lacquer box painted with astronomical patterns on its top, including the names of the lunnar mansions, valuable data for the research of the history of Chinese ancient astronomy. Because all the bronzes are inscribed with "Marquis Yi of Zeng", he must be the owner of the grave. At the same time, a *pu* bell made by the Kingdom of Chu has also been unearthed; it is dated "56th year reign of King Huiwang of Chu (433 B.C.)" and was given to the Marquis of Zeng, which proves that the funeral took place no earlier than 433 B.C. The discovery of this grave raised disputes on the enigma of the marquis state. Because in ancient records there in no mention of the state of Zeng and in the Eastern Zhou period, Suizhou belonged to the Sui state, further added with the fact that repeated finds of bronzes from this region and even from farther Xinye County, Henan Province, all were marked with Zeng; therefore Zeng and Sui might have been the same state. But others opine that they were two states. A consensus of opinion hasn't been reached.

(15) Tombs of the Zhongshan Kingdom (excavated 1974-78)

The finds of these tombs render important data for the study of the history of the Zhongshan Kingdom of the later stage of the Warring States, because in existing records the kingdom has not been noted in detail. The site is at the foot of the Lingshan Hills to the north of Pingshan Count, Hebei Province. Two tombs of two places have been excavated and have been numbered 1 and 6 respectively: All graves were sealed by thick

The gold and silver inlaid bronze tiger-devouring-a-fawn
unearthed from the tomb of the Zhongshan Kingdom

rammed earth up to the ground level, on which memo-
rial halls were built. Near the mausoleum are accompanying burials and pits of chariots and horses. The
layout of the coffin chamber is like the character *zhong*
(中) between two south-to-north passages. The square
coffin chamber is in the middle, but had been robbed;
only bronze ornaments of the coffin were left. Because
the burial articles had been placed in the flank storage
pits, they are still well preserved. No. 1 Tomb has
three storage pits while No. 6 has two. Burials were
unearthed of up to more than 19,000 pieces, consisting
of bronze objects, pottery, jade articles, lacquer wares,

etc. Other burials unearthed are horses, chariots, dogs, sheep, etc. Among the bronzes are a *shan* (山) shaped article over 1 metre high; another one which might represent the sovereignty; a square bronze table inlaid with gold and silver; a linked lamp with 15 lampwicks; a bronze tiger devouring a fawn, inlaid with gold and silver; a two-winged legendary beast inlaid with silver; all are exquisitely made precious artifacts. Most precious are the three pieces from Tomb No. 1—a tripod and two pots, inscribed with a total of 1,101 words, by which it is determined that the dead man was King Xi, one of the four kings of the Zhongshan Kingdom. The burials possess intense factors of the Central Regions, yet they have unique characteristics of their own, which is of great significance in making further study of the culture of the Zhongshan Kingdom.

(16) Tonglushan Ancient Mining and Smelting Site (excavated since 1973)

In the presence of such beautiful ancient bronzes, one would naturally like to know how the ancient artisans conducted their mining and smelting productions, but materials on this never existed before the finds of Tonglushan hillock, on a plain 3 kilometres to the northwest of Daye County, Hubei Province. In the excavation, ancient installations of vertical shafts, level shafts, blind shafts and inclined shafts have been unearthed, thus the distribution and connections of shafts are known to the public. For security of operation, wooden supports were employed in the shafts. One of the groups of three vertical shafts is surrounded

The whole view of the Tonglushan Ancient Mining
and Smelting Site

by 7 level shafts, in the shape of a fan; in the bottom
of the level shafts there are 7 blind wells with drainage
of wooden grooves. Here the ancient shafts were sunk
in two periods of time, the earlier belonged to the
Spring and Autumn Period (770-476 B.C.) or a little earlier; the later belonged to the Warring States
(475-221 B.C.) until the Western Han Dynasty (206
B.C.-A.D. 24).

The windlass had been employed for lifting ores or
conveying equipment at least since the Warring States
epoch. In the earlier stage, excavating appliances such
as hatchet, chisel, hoe, drill, etc., were made from
bronze while those of the later stage were made from
iron. Wooden spades; bamboo and rattan baskets for
loading; wooden windlass, ropes and wooden hooks for

lifting; wood grooves, barrels, dippers and boat-like buckets for draining, have also been unearthed. Besides, 8 vertical furnaces for smelting copper have been discovered, with their bases below the ground surface. Drafting channels were built in the middle of the furnace. Through simulated tests, we know such a vertical furnace was used for the reduction smelting of the oxidized ores; it could be continuously fed, drain slag continuously, and intermittantly release copper. Such a furnace is durable and easy to operate. Around the furnace, column pits of work sheds built then are still visible on the site. Stone hammering blocks for breaking ores, stone balls, processed ores, copper lumps, pottery daily-living utensils as well as a large quantity of slags were also found. All of these reflect the smelting technology of the time.

(17) Bamboo Slips of the Qin Dynasty (excavated 1975)

At Shuihudi (The Place Where the Tiger Slept), Yunmeng County, Hubei Province, there are scattered many graves of the Qin Dynasty, from which were unearthed a lot of bronzes, lacquer wares, pottery, bamboo and wood articles and other burial objects. Among them, the most precious are the more than 1,100 bamboo slips from Tomb No. 11. The grave owner was 40-year-old prison-officer Xi, buried in the 30th year of Emperor Qin Shi Huang's reign (217 B.C.). The slips were in the coffin, in 8 heaps, by the right side of the skull, belly and feet; they are basically well preserved. The slips are 23.1-27.8 centimetres long, held together with three strings on the top, centre and bottom; they were written with black ink in the *Li* style (official script) of the Qin Dynasty, still distinct and distinguishable.

The contents of the slips consist of 9 topics concerning the law and documents of the Qin Dynasty: *Bian Nian Ji (Annals Records), Eighteen Kinds of Laws of the Qin, Yu Shu (The Wording Book), Notes on the Law of the Qin, Questions and Answers of the Law, Feng Zhen Shi* (封珍式), *The Way to Be an Officer* and *Ri Shu* (日书). Though not the complete Qin law, yet the slips contained criminal law, procedural law, civil law, military law, administrative law, economic legislation, etc. All of these have great value in the study of the development of the ancient Chinese legal system. Among ancient Chinese laws, only the Tang Law has been well preserved until today. The find of the present slips is not only a great event in the history of the ancient Chinese legal system, but also of great importance to that of the world.

(18) Warrior and Horse Pits Surrounding Qin Shi Huang's Tomb (excavated since 1974)

Qin Shi Huang's Tomb is the first emperor's mausoleum in Chinese history. The tomb was built at the foot of Lishan Hills to the east of Lintong County seat, Shaanxi Province. The pottery figurine pits are at the north side of the road leading to the east gate of the mausoleum. Four of the pits have been discovered, covering an area of 25,380 square metres. The whole gallery was built as a log and earth structure. Pit No.

Pottery figurine unearthed from
the tomb of Qin Shi Huang

1 is the biggest, oblong in shape; Pit No. 2 is to its
northeast, in carpenter's square shape; Pit No. 3 is
smaller, to the northwest of Pit No. 1, in the shape of
the Chinese character *Ao* (凹); Pit No. 4 is between
No. 2 and No. 3, also in rectangular shape. It is an
empty pit, abandoned before it was finished.

For the time being, only Pit No. 3 has been fully
excavated. Added with a small part of Pits No. 1
and 2, a total area of 2,516 square metres has been
unearthed. From this part alone, 800 warriors, 18
wooden chariots, 100 horses and 9,000 bronze weapons,
chariots and horses have been unearthed. According to

the ancient battle array of troops, in the three pits there should be at least 7,000 soldiers, 100 four-horsed chariots, and more than 100 pottery warhorses. The height of figurines is about 1.8 metres, the same as humans; horses and chariots are also of true sizes. Facial features, coiffures, clothes and armour are all sculptured and coloured true to life; most weapons are real bronze weapons. All of these real objects afford precious data to the research of the arms, establishments and equipment of the Qin troops, at the same time reflecting the level of sculpture of the time. A museum has been established on the Pits for visitors from home and abroad, who are dumbfounded at the sight of the pottery troops in battle array and can't help admiring the miracle of the ancient Chinese culture.

(19) The Site of Chang'an City of the Han Dynasty (excavated since 1956)

The Western Han city is 3 kilometres to the northwest of present Xi'an City, Shaanxi Province. Through a long investigation, it has become clear that the city is somewhat square in shape, with curvatures along the south and north walls. The south wall is 7,600 metres long, the north wall 7,200 metres, the east wall 6,000 metres and the west wall 4,900 metres. The inner area of the city is about 36 square kilometres. The walls were built of rammed earth, and the thickness of the foundation is 12-16 metres. Surrounding the city are protecting ditches 8 metres wide and 3 metres deep. There are 3 gates on each wall, a total of 12 gates; each gate has 3 doorways.

Palaces and armouries inside the city have also been excavated. At the southeast corner, the length of the surrounding walls of the Changle Palace (The Ever-Happy Palace) is over 10,000 metres; the whole palace covers an area of 6 square kilometres, one sixth of the city area. At the southwest of the city is the site of Weiyang Palace, which is square in shape, surrounded by enclosing walls of a total length of 8,800 metres. Its area is about 5 square kilometres, covering one seventh of the city area. Between palaces are the armouries, which are enclosed by walls; both east and west walls are 320 metres, south and north walls 880 metres.

Foundations of seven of the armouries have been excavated. The largest one is 230 metres long and 46 metres wide, and partitioned into 4 rooms; wooden frames for storing arms are placed in the room. They have decayed, however, the remnants of base stones are still well arranged in rows. Guigong Palace (by the north of Weiyang Palace) and Jianzhang Palace (outside the west city) have also been excavated. Investigation has also been made on the Jiu Shi (Nine Markets) inside the city. Coin-moulds and pottery figurines have been found scattered on the ground, reflecting that workshops existed on this spot. In the south suburbs Pi Yong (the Imperial University) and Jiu Miao (Nine Temples) have been probed; the site of Pi Yong is a rounded rammed-earth terrace whose diameter is 62 metres, 30 centimetres above the ground level. Wang Mang's Nine Temples is a cluster site of 12 buildings, all of the same shape as the above-mentioned Pi Yong. The excavation testifies that Chang'an City, the city gates, palaces, armouries and the ritual constructions outside the south city, were all ruined in the flames of war during the end of Wang Mang's Xin Dynasty or a little later than that period.

(20) Mawangdui Han Tombs (excavated 1972, 1973-74)

Three tombs were excavated 4 kilometres east of the suburbs of Changsha City, Hunan Province; from Tomb 2, three seals were found: "Prime Minister of Changsha", "Seal of Marquis Dai" and "Li Cang". He died in the 2nd year of Han Emperor Huidi's reign (193 B.C.). Tomb 1 is abreast the east side of Tomb 2, in which is a 50-year-old female; she might have been Li Cang's wife. Tomb 3 is a 30-year-old male, who might have been the son of the marquis. All graves are in earth pits; No. 1 and No. 3 are better preserved. No. 1 has 4 coffins; the outmost is plain black-lacquered, the second coffin is flowered black-lacquered, the third is florated on crimson ground and the innermost coffin has feathers on a background of floral brocades, which is very beautiful. Through 2,100 years, the female corpse and its viscera are still freshly preserved, indeed a miracle in the medical history of the world. Tomb 3 has three coffins, but the corpse is not well preserved. Both inner coffins are covered by large T-shaped silk paintings with the theme of "Guiding the soul to ascend to heaven", which are precious ancient artifacts.

Immense numbers of burial objects were unearthed from these two graves; they are mainly various silk clothes, fine lacquer wares, bamboo chests full of provisions and medicines, musical instruments, bamboo and wood wares, pottery, bamboo slips and a large quantity of wooden figurines. In Tomb 3 were discovered many books copied on rolls of silk as well as two rolls on medical science. The silk rolls are *Lao Zi* (*Book of the Taoists*), *Zhou Yi* (*The Book of Changes*), *The Spring and Autumn Annals*, *Books of the Political Strategists in the Warring States Period*, *Fifty Two Medical Prescriptions*; in all, 28 kinds of books, totalling more than 120,000 words. Also unearthed were a coloured painting, "Dao Yin Tu" (Portrait of Guiding), and two ancient maps. One is "the Topographic Map of the Southern Part of the Changsha Princedom" and the other is "the Garrison Map"; they are the oldest maps existing in China. Therefore the finds of Mawangdui Han Tombs offer significant real object materials to the research of the development of the handicraft industry and the science and technology in the early stage of the Western Han Dynasty, as well as the history, culture and social life of the time.

(21) Mancheng Han Tombs (excavated 1968)

At Mancheng County of Hebei Province, caverns were made by chiselling rocks to a certain depth in the mountains. Tomb 1 is 51.7 metres long and partitioned into six sections—the tomb passage, the path, the south side-room, the north side-room, the central room and the back room. Tomb 2 is 49.7 metres long and in the same pattern. Both bodies were buried in the back room and placed in jade shrouds. Because bronzes from Tomb 1 are all inscribed with "the Imperial Storehouse of the Zhongshan Princedom" and documents

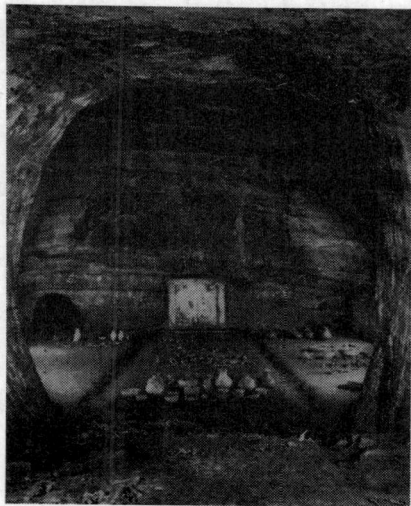

The excavation of the central chamber of
Liu Sheng's tomb at Mancheng

are sealed with "the Imperial Officer of the Zhongshan Princedom", the body must have been one of the princes. The numbering of years on the bronzes and lacquer wares are all over thirty years, therefore Liu Sheng must be the owner of the Tomb, because among the princes he was the only one who had reigned over Zhongshan for more than thirty years; he died in Yuanding the 4th Year (113 B.C.). Bronzes from Tomb 2 are also inscribed with "Zhongshan Storehouse" and a copper seal "Dou Wan", therefore the tomb owner must be Liu Sheng's wife, Dou Wan. The two tombs were prepared at the same time although the bodies were separately interred. Both jade shrouds are well preserved. The total number of burials unearthed is more than 4,200 pieces, among which, a "Changle Palace" lamp, a gold inlaid burner, a gold-and-silver-inlaid and seal-character-inscribed bird bronze pot, a gilded silver-inlaid nipple-designed bronze pot, a jade-handled steel sword, a suit of iron armour, two sets of curtain hooks, a bronze water clock as well as a bronze basin carved with "the Medical Workshop" are all rare relics, rendering valuable real object data to the research of the histories of medical, astronomical and natural sciences of the time.

(22) The Beacon-fire Site of the Han Dynasty at Juyan (excavated 1972-76)

Juyan Beacon-fire Site is on the reaches of Ejina River in Inner Mongolia, where, in the beginning of the 30's, large numbers of slips were discovered. At this time, three different types of sites have been excavated. They are respectively Jiaquhouguan (Pochengzi), Jiaquzhai No. 4 Beacon-fire Site and the site of Jianshuijinguan, totalling an area of 4,500 square metres. The site of Jiaquhouguan is the largest. Slips alone unearthed from these three sites totalled 19,637, in addition to the volumes of compiled documents, arrowheads, weapons, farming tools, cereals, fishing and hunting articles, seals, sealing-clay, writing brushes, inkslabs, rulers as well as pieces of paper made from jute fibres. The number of slips excavated to this time is the largest found; they furnish references in the study of the politics, economy, military science, nationalities and social life of the Han Dynasty.

(23) The Site of Luoyang City of the Han Dynasty and the Kingdom of Wei (excavated 1962)

The site is 15 kilometres to the east of the City of Luoyang, Henan Province, which had been the capital of the Eastern Han Dynasty, Cao's Kingdom of Wei, the Western Jin and the Northern Wei Dynasty. Excavation work started in 1962. The Eastern Han's Luoyang City was rectangular in shape, with a circumference about 13,000 metres long; the

The remnants of the east wall of the Han, Wei Luoyang City

rammed-earth foundations of walls are 14-25 metres thick. The whole city has 12 gates, three each on the east and west, four on the south and two on the north side.

The ruins of the Royal College, the Sacrificial Hall, the Astronomical Observatory and the Imperial Academy of the Eastern Han Dynasty have also been excavated. The observatory is on the west side of the main road outside the south part of the city. It is square in shape, surrounded by walls. A 50-metre-square terrace was built in the middle, the remnant of which is about 8 metres high. Around it rooms were built; the lower floor has corridors and the upper floor has five rooms on each side paved with rectangular bricks. The back walls are pasted in green, white, red and black according to the directions east, west, south and north respectively, representing the symbols of orientation: the Green Dragon, the White Tiger, the Red Bird and the Black Tortoise. This building had been continually used by the Kingdom of Wei and the Western Jin Dynasty, but by the end of the latter dynasty it was heavily destroyed by the flames of war, and was finally abandoned during the Northern Wei Dynasty. The site of the Imperial Academy has also been investigated, and remnants of Stone Classics have been found in the ruins.

Luoyang City was rebuilt on the ruins of the Han's city by the Kingdom of Wei. The layout was about the same as before, but the Jinrong City was added to it at the northwest corner. The small city was divided into three parts; as it was a military castle, all of the gateways opened onto each other, north to south 1,080 metres and west to east 250 metres long.

During the Northern Wei Dynasty, Luoyang City was still the same as before; only the 12 gates had been rebuilt and renamed. The Xiyang Gate of the west city was removed slightly northward. All of the other gates remained intact; however, a new gate was opened on the west city wall, totalling 13 gates. The main alteration of the city was to convert it solely to palace use: rectangular in shape, surrounded by walls, west and east 1,400 metres, north and south both 660 metres. The main palace, Taiji Dian, is in the fore part of the city; its foundation north to south is 60 metres, west to east is 100 metres; the palace must have been very magnificent. Eight of the main streets have been found out, each criss-crossing four other streets. The third cross street is as wide as 40-42 metres and is just on the central axis of communication, therefore it must be the Street of the Bronze Camel.

There were many famous Buddhist monasteries in the city, but for the time being, only the Yongning Monastery has been discovered. Its surrounding walls is 1,060 metres long. The central square pagoda base still exists there, 5 metres above the ground level; two storeys are still left. When the pagoda base was cleared, many stone sculptures, eaves tiles and building materials as well as many exquisite remnants of clay sculptures were found. Among them were about 300 Buddhas, monks, civil officers, warriors, and male and female attendants, exquisitely made. From these excavated objects, it is not hard for us to imagine how magnificent the pagoda looked, as noted in the *Notes on the Luoyang Buddhist Monasteries* (*Luo Yang Qie Lan Ji*).

(24) Shizhaishan Dian Graves
(excavated 1955-60)

The graves are at Shizhaishan, Jinning County, Yunnan Province. After four excavations, 48 graves have been unearthed, along with more than 4,000 burial objects. From Grave 6, a snake-knobbed golden chop bearing the negative impression of "the Seal of the King of Dian" was discovered, as a result, the graves have been determined to be graves of the Dians. The graveyard had been employed for quite a long time, from the later age of the Warring States up to the

Wolf-devouring-deer hollow-sculptured bronze ornament unearthed from the Shizhaishan Dian Graves

early Eastern Han Dynasty. All of the graves are vertical earth pits without any earth sealing on the ground surface. Some are coffined, most are single graves, but the wood and human bones have decayed away. A few of the bodies are shrouded with pearled attire made by joining agate, soft-jade or turquoise together with metal wire. Among the funeral objects, most are bronzes, added with weapons, ritual articles, implements, vessels and ornaments. Particularly noteworthy are those large bronze cowrie containers with portraits of war or sacrificial service carved on the lids. The make of weapons also has its national characteristics, often adorned with images of birds and beasts. Of the bronze articles, some are adorned with scenes of war or the taking of captives; on bronze spears there are naked hanging figures, indicating that the Dians were still under the slave system. Iron tools had appeared, although weapons proper were still bronze; only the edge was inserted with iron. As time passed, more iron tools arose. Their make became more like that of the Central Regions, also reflecting that the Han Dynasty had reinforced the control of their frontiers.

(25) The Wangs' Graves at Xiangshan, Nanjing (excavated 1965-70)

The excavation of the Wangs' Graves is an important archaeological discovery of the Kingdom of Wei, the Jin Dynasty and the Northern and Southern Dynasties. Xiangshan is commonly called Rentaishan, a kilometre outside the Xinmin Gate in the northern

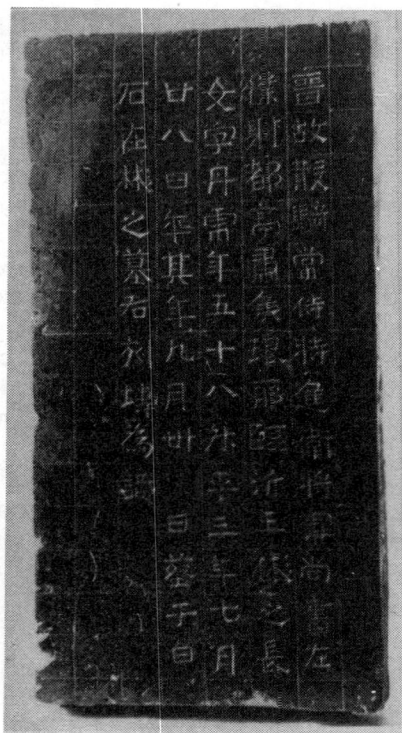

Wang Danhu's brick epitaph unearthed from the Wangs'
Graves at Xiangshan, Nanjing

suburbs of Nanjing. During 1965-70, seven graves were
cleared; except for Grave 2, the remainder are of the
Eastern Jin Dynasty. Four of them have stone or brick
epitaphs: Wang Xingzhi's stone epitaph, dated Xian-
kang 7th Year (341), and on the back of the same stone

is his wife Song Hezhi's epitaph dated Yonghe 4th Year; Wang Minzhi's brick epitaph dated Shengping Second Year (358); Wang Danhu's brick epitaph dated Shengping 3rd Year (359); Wang Bin's wife Xia Jinhu's brick epitaph dated Taiyuan 17th Year (392). Through all these we are convinced that these are the graves of the noted Langya (prefecture) Wangs.

In addition to the epitaphs, unearthed were a lot of celadons, pottery, bronzes, gold and silver ornaments, amber beads, colour-glazed beads, crystal beads, and turquoise beads, as well as imported glass cups, diamond rings, etc. In Wang Danhu's grave there is a lacquer case containing 200 pills which have been tested; their main component is mercuric sulphide. All of these finds provide valuable real object materials for the research of the funeral customs of the aristocratic families of the Eastern Jin Dynasty, the social life, and the technological level of the time. The style of writing of the epitaphs are also important in the study of the history of the development of ancient Chinese calligraphy.

(26) The Northern Wei Tombs at Datong (excavated 1965, 1976)

Datong City of Shanxi Province was the capital Pingcheng of the Northern Wei Dynasty, where many important tombs were placed. Among them were the Tomb of Sima Jinlong and the Yongguling Tomb of the Queen of Fangshan Wenming. Sima Jinlong was a royal prince of the Western Jin who surrendered to the Northern Wei and died in Taihe the 8th year (484); his tomb, found in Shijiazhai Village, Datong City, and excavated in 1965-66, was a multi-roomed brick tomb, with "Tomb-bricks of the Tomb of the Prince of Lang-ya, Shima Jinlong" inscribed on the bricks. Co-buried in the same tomb was his wife, Ji Chen, who died in Yanxing the 4th year (747). The tomb had been disturbed and robbed, yet a large amount of pottery figurines and daily appliances still existed. There were as many as 400 pieces of figurines and animal models, half of which were armoured infantry and cavalry as well as horses and camels bearing provisions; some of the soldiers had the look of minorities. In the back chamber there were still retained a finely carved stone

Armoured cavalry pottery figurine unearthed from Shima Jinlong's Tomb at Datong

bed and parts of a lacquer screen and its stone-carved base. Portraits of women of character were painted on separate leaves with brilliant colouring and lively strokes, a few words written on each picture to explain the stories of the women; it is a rare artifact of the ancient time. Besides, stone inkslabs, pottery pots, celadon spittoon, lacquered partition board, iron scissors, stirrups, etc., have also been unearthed.

Fangshan Yonggu Tomb, cleared in 1976, is situated 25 kilometres to the north of the Datong City. On the square tomb base, the sealing earth is as high as 22.87 metres. In front of the tomb is the remnant of a square pagoda base surrounded by a corridor, ahead of which is a rectangular building site. It is evident that the tomb was built together with the Buddhist monastery; the layout is full of Buddhist colouring. It is a pity that the tomb had long since been robbed; the remarks written in 1156-61 (the reign of Zhenglong of the Kin Dynasty) are still left in the tomb, but all of the funeral objects had been taken away. Only remnants of stone figurines, iron spears, iron arrowheads, small glass cups and fragments of pottery are still left in the tomb. However, the traces of construction of the tomb are still detectable; comprised of the tomb path, the front chamber, the passageway and the main chamber, its total length is 23.5 metres. The main chamber is square in shape but four walls are slightly convex, then contracted on the top to form a central pointed square roof with a white sandstone-sculptured lotus flower placed on top of it. At the ends of the passageway are stone gates. The doorframes and the niche columns are relief-sculptured with designs of lotus petals; on the columns at two sides are carved a Red

Bird holding pearls in its beak and a barefoot boy holding flower buds with both hands, in lively posture and with a sweet look. All of these were meticulously wrought, having the highest artistic value, peerless among the Northern Wei sculptures.

(27) Brick Mosaics in the Tombs of the Southern Dynasties at Danyang (excavated 1965, 1968)

King's tombs of the Southern Dynasties are concentrated at Danyang County, Jiangsu Province, and

Brick mosaics unearthed from
the tombs of the Southern Dynasties at Danyang

there are many fine funeral stone sculptures still existing above the ground surface. Within three years, three large-scale brick tombs have been excavated, but all of them had been robbed, that is why there are very few burials unearthed. But the construction of the tombs and the brick mosaics on the tomb walls are still well preserved. Due to the dense moisture in the south, frescoes could hardly be retained; therefore this type of brick mosaic artifact was employed in place of frescoes. First a draft of the picture was made, then the position of each brick was marked and finally they were laid on the wall. Some of the mosaics are 2.5 metres long. The subject matters are quite varied; there are the images of dragon, tiger, lion, armoured warriors, cavalry, guards with halberds and bands with drumbeats and pipeblowing, etc. Most splendid are the Seven Sages in the Bamboo Grove of the Kingdom of Wei and the Jin Dynasty, and the portraits of Rong Qiqi and the other seven figures. Generally on the side walls of the passageway between the gate and the gravechamber 8 or 10 pairs of mosaic pictures of different sizes are symmetrically placed. The pictures are in graceful lines and vivid, having very high artistic value, leaving a gap for you to have a peep at the true features of the Chinese painting in the Six Dynasties (Wu, Eastern Jin, Song, Qi, Liang and Chen).

(28) The Ruins of Chang'an City of the Tang Dynasty (excavated since 1957)

Chang'an City of the Tang Dynasty was a famous influential city of the world. The excavation and exploration work of it has been conducted since 1957 and is continuing up to now. The layout of the outer city, the palace city, the imperial household city and the streets has been scientifically determined. The outer city is rectangular, east and west 9,721 metres, north and south 8,651.7 metres, perimeter 36.7 kilometres. City walls were built by rammed earth, only bricked at gates, 12 metres thick and surrounded by ditches. There are three gates on each side, each with three doorways, only the Mingdemen has five doorways. Within the outer walls in the middle of the north part of the city are the palace city and the imperial household city; the right and left of the north and the southern part of the city are intersected by lanes; at the southeast and the southwest of the Imperial City are the East and the West Markets. It was a standard Chinese street-and-lane type closed city, tidily projected and compact. Inside the outer city there were 11 north to south streets, 14 west to east streets. The central street north to south was the Red Bird Street which is 150-155 metres wide and raised in the middle; by the sides are escape ditches 3.3 metres wide. The whole city was partitioned into 110 *fangs* (blocks), generally the *fangs* were closed but doors were opened at four sides and crisscross streets are opened in the *fangs*. Buddhist monasteries were scattered everywhere in the city. The famous Mi-School Buddhist Rite has been excavated, the remains of pagoda and halls have been found. The commercial centres, the East and West Markets have also been investigated; remains of shops, maybe provision shops, jewellers and workshops have been found. Daming Palace and Xingqing Palace have been excavated. Daming Palace's layout is rectangular in the southern part but trapezoidal in the north, with a total area of about 3.2 square kilometres. More than 40 traces of buildings have been found, mostly in the northern part of the palace city. Halls of Hanyuandian, Lindedian, where dinners were given to courtiers, and the Taoists' Sanqingdian have been excavated. The site of Hanyuandian is 15 metres above ground level; the existing foundation base is 75.9 metres east to west, 41.3 metres north to south; the Hall is 11 bays wide and 4 rooms deep. To the southeast of the Hall is the Xianglan Pavilion, to the southwest is Xifeng Pavilion; winding corridors joined them together. In front of the Hall there are three parallel ways leading to the south, stone and brick paved alternately in stairs and slopes to a length of 78 metres, called Long Wei Dao (Dragon Tail Ways). The whole structure was magnificent.

(29) Tombs of Princess Yongtai, Prince Zhanghuai and Prince Yide (excavated 1960-62, 1971)

All of the three royal offspring died during the reign of the woman emperor Wu Zetian. Both Yide and his younger sister Yongtai were clubbed to death; Zhanghuai was banished to Bazhou (Sichuan) and later committed suicide. After Tang Emperor Zhongzong regained his throne, in the Second year of Shenlong (706), the brothers and sister were reburied to accompany the Qianling Mausoleum. Each of the three graves had a huge mound of sealing earth, an enclosing wall and a pair of earth watch-columns, in front of which there were stone sculptures. All three tombs had

Pottery cavalry figurines unearthed from the tomb
of Prince Yide of the Tang Dynasty

been robbed, but the construction of the underground
grave chambers is still well retained; particularly the
coloured frescoes are still well preserved. The three
tombs all have front and back chambers joined by a
passageway; before the grave chamber there is a long
passage which has many skylights, passage channels
and small shrines. The bodies were buried in the back
chamber, with a beautifully carved stone outer coffin,
but the wood coffin and the skeleton exist no more.

Most magnificent are the frescoes in Yide's tomb,
on the east and west walls of the passage; taking three
watch-columns and the city walls as background, rows
of walking and riding guards of honour and three
carriages were painted. The passage channel was painted with tamed leopards, attendants with falcons, men

and women servants; the skylights were painted with stands for halberds and imperial carriages; the passage leading to the gravechamber has maidservants carrying things; on the ceiling of the back chamber are the sun, the moon, the Milky Way and constellations.

The Zhanghuai Tomb's frescoes have the most life-like appeal; on the east wall is a portrait of hunting and on the west wall, playing ball, as well as officials leading foreign chieftains to the court. In the passage are painted men and women attendants carrying articles in their hands; on the west wall of the front chamber is a portrait of watching a bird catching a cicada; on the east wall of the back chamber are beautiful young women of the court. Among them, the ball playing on horseback is most vivid and touching, its brushing very graceful, indeed a masterpiece.

In Yongtai's tomb, except for the blue dragon, white tiger, guards of honour, halberd stands and the astronomical phenomena in the back chamber, all of the pictures are the imperial maids of honour with articles in their hands, particularly the group of girls on the east wall of the front chamber; its painting technique was most skillful, topmost among the Tang frescoes unearthed. Although the tombs had been robbed, their epitaphs were all well preserved; at the same time, those tricoloured pottery figurines, utensils, models and gold-gilded horse ornaments, gold flowers, etc., originally set in the small shrines are still in good condition. Most singled-out and characteristic is the mould for making a gold-gilded armoured cavalry figurine in Yide's tomb. In the same grave are the 11 slabs of marble inscriptions on the life of the Prince; the carvings are deep-set below the surface and gold-filled, written in regular script. The excavation of these three tombs provided materials for the study of the Tang royal family funeral system, and also had great significance in the research of Tang frescoes and the development of tricoloured pottery.

(30) Two Tombs of the Southern Tang (excavated 1950)

Both tombs are at the southern foot of the Gaoshan Hill to the northwest of Dongshan Town of Jiangning County, Jiangsu Province; the construction and scope

Stone sculptured warriors in Li Bian's Tomb
of the Southern Tang

are similar—both have front, middle and back chambers. By the sides of the front and middle chambers there are 4 flank rooms; on the four walls of the back chamber small niches are opened. The Southern Tang rule existed just 39 years (937-975). The tomb's front and middle chambers of the first king Li Bian were built of bricks while the back was of stones; the tomb of the second king Li Jing was completely made of bricks in the shape of wood, which had been coloured-painted. In Li Bian's tomb, at two ends on the northern wall of the middle chamber there was sculptured a pair of armoured warriors poking a sword to the ground with both hands; above that there was carved a pair of flying dragons playing with a burning pearl between them, the carving is exquisite but not so lively. In the back chamber of both graves there is a stone bed for the coffin and on the ceiling are painted astronomical phenomena, but coffins and bones exist no more. Because the graves had long since been robbed, only a small amount of remnant pottery, celadon wares and white porcelain bowls are still left. In Li Bian's tomb there are 23 pieces of jade lament slips; in Li Jing's tomb, 40 stone lament slips. Unearthed from two tombs were a total of 190 pieces: some of the figurines gave a good description of the imperial courtiers, their posture and their attire; other pottery like the tomb-dragon and the ritual-fish was mere superstitious funeral objects. The excavation of these two tombs of the southern separatist small regime provided important materials for the study of the funeral system of the Tang and Song dynasties.

(31) King Meng Zhixiang's Tomb of the Later Shu (excavated 1971)

Next to the excavation of King Wang Jian's tomb of the Earlier Shu (891-925), this tomb is at the southern foot of the Mopanshan Hill in the northern suburb 7 kilometres from Chengdu City, Sichuan Province. The tomb was built of green stones, but its construction was rather unique—three arch-roofed chambers abreast, with the diameter of the middle main chamber only 6.7 metres and the diameter of flank rooms only 3.4 metres, joined together by a paved path. The ground of the grave chamber was also flag paved. In front of the main chamber was a roofed path, the fore part of which is the grave passage of 22 slab-paved stairs. The path was fitted with stone gates and built with drainage works. The gates were made imitating the construction of wood; two ends of the ridge are adorned with sea-beasts, dragons and phoenixes. On the coloured columns are carved a green dragon and a white tiger, and by their sides stand a pair of armoured warriors 1.1 metres tall. In the grave chamber there are murals of men and women attendants. The coffin was placed on a mountain-shaped stone bed, but the wood coffin and the body exist no more, only the stone bed is still in good condition. The stone bed is 5.1 metres long, 2.1 metres high, and divided into 3 layers. On the lower layer are sculptured naked men of great strength, kneeling and bearing with their shoulders; on the middle layer there are pole holes for spreading the coffin canopy, and armoured warriors by the four corners; the four sides of the upper layer are carved with dragons playing with a pearl; the sculpturing was very fine. Because the tomb had long since been robbed, only at the right side in front of the stone bed are there an epitaph and a stone vat, and at the left side some broken jade lament slips are found. The epitaph belonged to Meng Zhixiang's wife, the Elder Princess of Fu Qing, the eldest daughter of Li Keyong, the Prince of Jin. The broken jade lament slips are inscribed with "Mingde the first year...", "the late king...", therefore they belong to Meng Zhixiang. The tomb of Meng Zhixiang, the tomb of Wang Jian and the two tombs of the Southern Tang offer good materials for the research of the funeral system of the Tang and Song dynasties.

(32) Song Graves at Baisha (excavated 1951)

Three chamber tombs of the Northern Song Dynasty at the north of Baisha Town, Yuxian County, Henan Province, were excavated in 1951. They were brick laid, imitating the construction of wood. From the First Tomb was unearthed a brick land-purchasing contract written in vermilion, dated Yuanfu the second year (1099); based on which Zhao Daweng and his family were the owners of the tombs. Zhao Daweng's tomb is the largest, with fore and back chambers connected by a passage having a total length of 7.26 metres. Before the tomb, the archway was built after wood construction; dougongs, eaves, rafters and ridges were all built of bricks and colour-painted. The front chamber is flat and square in shape, and the ceiling is colour-painted; the rear chamber is hexagonal and the top cover is pointed up in the centre. The walls, pillars

Frescoes in a Song Tomb at Baisha

and brackets are laid with bricks and colour-painted. The passage, front chamber and back chamber are full of frescoes; on the walls there are attendants bearing strings of coins, with tubular stakes and wine bottles in hands, and leading a horse. By the sides of the gate are warriors; on the east wall are 11 female musicians playing for the tomb owners feasting on the opposite wall. On the northwest and northeast walls of the back chamber are brick-laid lattice windows; on the south-west wall is a woman wearing a coronet before a mirror; on the southeast wall are men and women servants carrying objects in their hands; on the north wall is a brick-carved woman trying to open a board door. In the back chamber there is a brick-laid coffin bed, on which were placed two reburied skeletons. Unearthed from the tomb was a vermilion-written brick land-purchasing contract, but very few burials, only a pair of small porcelain bowls, a piece of copper currency stamped "Shao Sheng Yuan Bao", some decayed iron wares, fragments of jars and porcelains. Judging from the contents of the tomb, the owner of the tomb might have been a landlord and concurrently a merchant. The other two tombs are abreast at the north of the First Tomb. Their constructions are simpler; both are flat hexagonal single-chamber brick-laid tombs, also imitating wood construction and painted with frescoes, but everything is much simpler than the tomb of Zhao Daweng.

(33) Kings' Tombs of the Western Xia Regime (1038-1227) (excavated 1972)

Kings' tombs of the Western Xia regime are scattered at the east foot of the Helanshan Mountains 25 kilometres west of Yinchuan City of the Ningxia Hui Autonomous Region. The whole graveyard covers 4 kilometres east to west, 10 kilometres north to south. The tombs are surrounded by rammed-earth walls into a flat rectangular huge mausoleum. Cemetery No. 8 has been excavated: on the south stand two watchtowers, between which is the passageway, at each side of which stands a tombstone covered by a shallow pavilion, but the stones had been broken. To the north of the tombstones are the outer walls, the small outer city and inner city. Burial articles do not exist any more, only some decayed gold and silver ornaments, iron wares, some copper armour scales and some fragments of pottery are still left. In Cemetery No. 2, near the tombstone, 511 fragments of Chinese character-inscribed stone pieces and 1,265 Western Xia character-carved stone pieces have been collected from the tomb. Through analysis, these might be useful in identifying the Western Xia language and in researching the history of the small regime. Apart from these, from other kings' tombs were also unearthed some gold-plated copper cattle, stone horse, stone dog, green glazed pottery pot, coins of the Northern Song Dynasty and tatters of silk fabrics. All of these may be useful to further archaeological excavation of these tombs and to the study of the history of the district regime established by the Dangxiang minority nationality of the time.

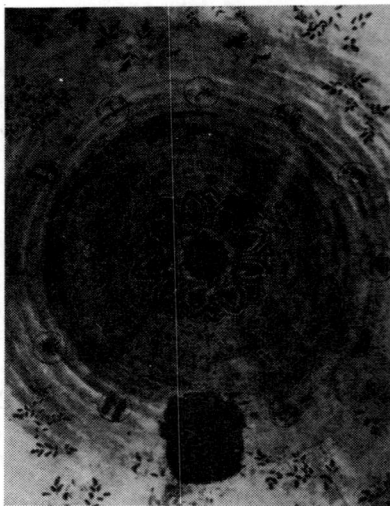

The Zodiac Picture in a Liao tomb at Xuanhua

(34) The Liao Tomb at Xuanhua (excavated 1974-75)

The Xuanhua Liao Tomb is noted for its zodiac picture on the arched roof of the back grave chamber. This is a brick tomb consisting of front and back chambers, discovered at Balicun Village, Xuanhua County, Hebei Province. According to the inscription of the tombstone in the back chamber, the grave owner, Zhang Shiqing, died in the Sixth Year of Tianqing (1116) of the Liao Dynasty. Four walls and the ceiling of the grave chamber are painted with coloured frescoes; among which the portrait of merry-making is the most vivid and lively—a dancer accompanied by a band of 12 musicians. On the walls of the back chamber are male and female servants attending the grave owner at a feast and reading the Buddhist scriptures; on the ceiling is the coloured zodiac picture. The arched roof is 2.17 metres in diameter, in the middle of which a bronze mirror is inserted, around which is a nine-petalled lotus flower; around the flower are the seven stars of the Big Dipper, the lunar mansions and other Chinese traditional stars. The background of the sky is bright blue in colour; stars are red dots connected by red straight lines. Beyond the lunar mansions are the Western imported but long Sinocized 12 signs of the zodiac; among them only the Taurus had been destroyed by the tomb robbers, others are still well preserved. What was different from the Western signs is that Virgo showed 2 girls instead of one, and moreover the girls are clad in ancient Chinese attire. Based on this find, the noted archaeologist Xia Nai concluded that the origin of the lunar mansions from Babylon was unfounded; that the theory China and Hindu were of the same origin might be true; but through further investigation, he decided that the origin was actually China.

(35) The Site of Dadu of the Yuan Dynasty (excavated 1964-67)

The site of the Yuan Dynasty, Dadu, is in the inner city of the present Beijing and a part of land to the north of the city. The site is rectangular in shape: its southern city wall is a little to the south of the present

Heyimen Gate and Wenchengmen Gate of Dadu City
of the Yuan Dynasty

East Chang'an Boulevard and West Chang'an Boulevard; the west and east walls just coincide with the present city walls; and the northern wall is on the line between Andingmen Xiaoguan and Deshengmen Xiaoguan. The whole city was built by rammed earch, with a wall base up to 24 metres thick; north to south 7,600 metres long; west to east about 6,700 metres, total area more than 50 square kilometres. At the same time, the scope of the imperial city and the palace city, the location of the central axis, the arrangement of streets and lanes, the distribution and the run of river and lake waters, have all been made clear. Some of the city gates, sewers and the dwelling sites have also been excavated.

In 1969, when removing the Shooting Tower of Xizhimen, Heyimen gate and Wengchengmen gate of Dadu of the Yuan Dynasty were discovered under the Shooting Tower. This is an important find, as in the gate mouth, an inscription of Zhizheng the 18th year (1358) was found. The gate tower had been removed when the Ming Dynasty gate was built on top of it, but the framework was still left, which measured 22 metres high; the inner arch was 6.68 metres high, outer, 4.56 metres; wooden door planks had been removed but the semicircular ironwork of the door bearing and the stone block of it were still left. On top of the archway there were stone-made fire-extinguishing appliances for pouring down water on the wooden planks in case of a fire alarm. More than ten dwelling sites have been excavated; those at Houyingfanghutong and behind the Yonghegong Monastery were better preserved. In the big residence at Houyingfanghutong, the main rooms in the main courtyard were built on a terrace-base with a wide corridor in the front and large chambers behind; and there were wing rooms by their east and west sides; in the east courtyard, north and south rooms were connected by pillared corridor, this character " I " shaped layout of construction was popular in the Song and Yuan dynasties. The site behind the Yonghegong Monastery was a three-combined compound, in which there was a brick-paved raised passageway leading to the main rooms and the east and west wing rooms. On the site of Xitiaohutong was discovered a construction something like a storehouse, from which were unearthed some porcelains, mother-of-

The Underground Palace of the Dingling Tomb of the Ming Dynasty

pearl inlaid lacquer wares, inkslabs, black and white Chinese chess pieces, etc.

(36) Dingling Underground Mausoleum of the Ming Dynasty (excavated 1956-58)

Dingling is the mausoleum of Emperor Wanli —Zhu Yijun, one of the 13 Ming Tombs situated at the foot of the Dayushan Mountains in the middle west part of the grave area. The underground palace was built under the sealing-mound in Baocheng Village, comprising 5 huge stone-built halls in 3 rows; by the sides of the central hall are side halls, with a total area up to 1,190 square metres. In the central hall there are 3 stone altars on which were placed five sacrificial vessels and a jar-like ever-burning lamp. In the back hall there is a stone-laid coffin bed, on which were placed the coffins of the emperor and his two wives (Empress Xiao Duan and Empress Xiao Jing); each was in an inner and an outer coffin, and all of the bodies had decayed. Over 3,000 pieces of various funeral objects were unearthed, a lot of them are exclusively used for emperor and empress, such as the emperor's golden crown, the jade tablet (*gui*), the ceremonial robe and the queen's phoenix coronet and a hundred-boys-designed queen's coat, etc., but the posthumous-title-grant and the title-chop set into the grave are not the real things but wooden facsimiles (both should be made of jade or gold). Apart from these, large lots of unearthed silk fabrics, gold and silver wares, jade wares and jewellery all have certain artistic value for the research of the technological level of the time.

197

Since the excavation, the Dingling Museum has been established and opened to public for visitors from home and abroad.

图书在版编目（CIP）数据

一座失踪王陵的发现：中国文物与考古专集/
杨泓等编著.—北京：外文出版社，1995
ISBN 7－119－01540－0

Ⅰ.一… Ⅱ.杨… Ⅲ.文物—考古—中国—文集
Ⅳ.K87－53

中国版本图书馆 CIP 数据核字（95）第 09625 号

一座失踪王陵的发现
—— 中国文物考古选集

＊

Ⓒ外文出版社

外文出版社出版
（中国北京百万庄路 24 号）
邮政编码 100037
外文印刷厂印刷
中国国际图书贸易总公司发行
（中国北京车公庄西路 35 号）
北京邮政信箱第 399 号　邮政编码 100044
1995 年(34 开)第一版
（英）
ISBN 7－119－01540－0 /G·85(外)
01380
7－E－2952P